A HANDBOOK OF
NORSE
MYTHOLOGY

KARL MORTENSEN

TRANSLATED FROM THE DANISH BY
A. CLINTON CROWELL

DOVER PUBLICATIONS, INC.
MINEOLA, NEW YORK

Bibliographical Note

This Dover edition, first published in 2003, is an unabridged republication of the work first published by Thomas Y. Crowell Company, New York, in 1913.

Library of Congress Cataloging-in-Publication Data

Mortensen, Karl, b. 1867.
    [Nordisk mythologi. English]
    A handbook of Norse mythology / by Karl Mortensen; translated from the Danish by A. Clinton Crowell.
       p. cm.
    "This Dover edition, first published in 2003, is an unabridged republication of the work first published by Thomas Y. Crowell Company, New York, in 1913."
    ISBN 0-486-43219-X (pbk.)
    1. Mythology, Norse. I. Crowell, A. Clinton (Asa Clinton) II. Title.

BL860.M613 2003
293'.13—dc21

                                  2003055145

Manufactured in the United States of America
Dover Publications, Inc., 31 East 2nd Street, Mineola, N.Y. 11501

Author's Preface

This popular presentation of the myths and sagas which took shape here in the North but whose foundation is common property of all the people who speak a Gothic-Germanic language, first appeared in 1898 and has been used since then in the study of Norse Mythology in the high schools and universities of all the Scandinavian countries. Since Professor Crowell has thought that the little book might also achieve a modest success in the youngest but richest and most powerful branch which has grown from our common root, I have without hesitation accepted his friendly proposal to translate it into English. I find great satisfaction in having my work put into the world's most comprehensive language and placed before students in the United States, where I have so many friends, where so many relatives and fellow-countrymen have found a home and a future, and toward which country we Northerners look with the deepest admiration and respect for the mighty forces which are seeking to control material things and to break new ground in the infinite realms of the intellect.

I sincerely thank Professor Crowell for his intelligent rendering of my Danish text, since on account of the nature of the subject and the half-poetic form, it has called for patient work and for uncommon insight. I would likewise thank the Thomas Y. Crowell Company of New York for their willingness to publish the book.

It is my earnest hope that the American student into whose hands the book may fall will be able to reap from it the advantage which the translator has had in mind and to feel awakened in him some of the love for our oldest common memorials, which has inspired the author in his task.

KARL MORTENSEN.

ODENSE, DENMARK
December, 1912.

Translator's Preface

The idea of translating Dr. Mortensen's *Nordisk Mythologi* suggested itself when my attention was called to the book by Professor E. Mogk of Leipzig.

I am chiefly indebted to the author, who has read the translation of all the prose and commented upon unusual points, all with friendly and cordial interest. With his consent I have translated the illustrative strophes from the Icelandic, according to the text of B. Sijmons in the *Germanistische Handbibliothek,* having for consultation H. Gering's *Vollständiges Wörterbuch der Edda,* the German translation of Gering, the Danish of Gjessing, and the English of some unpublished selections by my friend, the late Dr. Adrian Scott, sometime member of the Brown University faculty. When the work was practically complete, I saw Olive Bray's more recent translation and was slightly influenced by it. Dr. H. Hermannsson of Cornell University has read my strophes, making corrections and suggestions. I thank him for his interest and encouragement, and I thank Professor A. Heusler of Berlin for many helpful hints. I have also been assisted in many ways by my wife, Carrie E. Crowell, A.M.

Professor W. H. Schofield's translation of Sophus Bugge's *The Home of the Eddic Poems* has been most valuable for reference, especially in the matter of spelling.

A. C. C.

PROVIDENCE, R. I.,
January, 1913.

Contents

FOURTH SECTION

General Introduction

1. By "Norse mythology" we mean the information we have concerning the religious conceptions and usages of our heathen forefathers, their faith and manner of worshiping the gods, and also their legends and songs about the gods and heroes. The importation of Christianity drove out the old heathen faith, but remnants or memories of it long endured in the superstitious ideas of the common people, and can even be traced in our own day.

There has never been found on earth a tribe of people which did not have some kind of religion, but the lower the plane of civilization on which the people are found, the ruder and less pleasing are their religious ideas. Religions consequently change and develop according as civilization goes forward. One can, therefore, learn much by knowing the mythology of a race, since it shows us what stage the people in question have attained in intellectual development, what they regard as highest and most important in life and death, and what they regard as good or evil.

Sun-worship and Nature-worship.—We can easily perceive that a belief in counseling and controlling gods presupposes a far higher civilization than savage people in their earlier history possess. Religious ideas proceed partly from soul belief, belief in the continued life of the soul, and partly from the belief that nature is something living, peopled by mysterious beings which control regular and irregular changes in nature upon which man feels himself dependent. Such beings are often designated by the Greek word *Demons*. These nature-demons make themselves plainly known through the roaring of the

1

storm, the rippling of the water, or the wind's gentle play with the tree-tops. But races in the childhood period of their development cannot hold fast to a belief in life apart from bodies. Demons, therefore, are thought of in bodily form—as men or beasts. At the same time man feels his helplessness and powerlessness in the presence of Nature and its mysterious forces; he is prompted, then, by offerings and supplications to gain friendly relations with these powers which he with his own strength cannot overcome. In this we begin to find the first germ of divine worship which is capable of subsequent development, since ever increasing domain is given to the single demon. With the advance of civilization there is developed in the place of the belief in demons a belief in mighty gods, who are thought of as beautiful and perfect human forms.

Greek and Norse Mythology.—With the more developed heathen people there is always an exact correspondence between the nature of the country, the character of the people, and their religious belief. There is, therefore, a striking distinction also between Greek and Norse mythology. The Greek is bright and pleasant, like the country itself; the gods are thought of as great and beautiful human forms who are extolled not merely as gods, with offering and worship, but also as inspired Greek artists and poets, producers of statues and songs, the equal of which the world has scarcely seen. Norse mythology as we know it from the latest periods of the heathen age is, on the contrary, more dark and serious, and when it lays the serious aside it often becomes rude in its jesting. Norsemen felt the lack of talent for the sculptor's and painter's art, although they were really clever in carving wood; their idols were as a rule merely clumsy wooden images embellished in various ways. Their religious faith, on the other hand, has called forth poetry which in its way is by no means inferior to the Greek; and our forefathers' view of death and particularly their teaching about Ragnarok, concerning which we shall speak later, can rightly be preferred to the Greeks' faith in a miserable shadowlife in a realm of death (Hades).

Why We Teach Norse Mythology.—For us Norse mythology has in any case the advantage of being the religion of our own forefathers, and through it we learn to know that religion. This is necessary if we wish to understand aright the history and poetry of our antiquity and to comprehend what good characteristics and what faults Christianity encountered when it was proclaimed in the North. Finally, it is necessary to know the most important points of the heathen faith of our fathers in order to appreciate and enjoy many of the words of our best poets. This is especially true concerning Oelenschlaeger and Gruntvig, who not only have embodied large parts of the Norse mythology in independent poetic works (as "The Gods of the North," "Earl Hakon," "Scene from the Conflict of the Norns and Aesir") but also often borrow from it in their other works terms and figures which we ought to be able to understand. To point to the antiquity of the North and to our fathers' faith, life, and achievements was one of the poet's principal means of awakening the slumbering national feeling at the beginning of our century.

2. *Oldest Inhabitants of the North.*—It is possible that it was our ancestors who, several thousand years before the Christian era, inhabited Scandinavia, in the stone age. Learned investigations have in every case proved as most probable and reasonable that people of the bronze age, both before and after the year 1000 B.C., belonged to the same race as the Northmen of the iron age, so that our heathen era stretches over a space of at least two thousand years. We must, therefore, seek information about the oldest religious ideas of the North in prehistoric archæology, the science which investigates and throws light upon every species of relic preserved from antiquity. Here it is especially burial rites and the placing in graves of objects supposed to be offerings which have mythological significance.

Fig. 1.—Round Barrows.

Fig. 2.—Long Barrows.

a. In the remains of the earliest stone age, the refuse heaps, no burial places have been discovered; but from the latest stone age have been found a great number of graves, round and long barrows, sepulchral chambers (Figs. 1–3), and stone "chests," in which bodies were laid unburned and supplied with the necessary implements, which shows a belief in a continued life after death. Burned places and remnants of pyres in the graves seem to indicate offerings to or for the dead, and hewn in the stones are often found certain saucer-like depressions, wheels and crosses, which most likely have religious significance (Fig. 4).

b. In the bronze age, which ends some hundred years before the birth of Christ, men long preserved burial rites from the stone age. Bodies were not burned, but were placed in raised mounds in a tightly closed stone setting or in chests of hollowed trunks of oaks. Later, however, the burning of bodies became more and more common; ashes were preserved in stone vessels or most often in clay urns within the mounds; many times use was made of old mounds from the stone age. The greatest number of our barrows contain, therefore, tombs from the bronze age (Figs. 5–7). The reason for this change in the mode of burial seems to be the rise of new ideas about life after death. At first people believed in a continued life of the body, later they burned the body to set free the soul. Likewise in the stone age men deposited in the graves sacrificial gifts, handsomely wrought objects for use or ornament. For decoration are used now also

Fig. 3.—Sepulchral Chambers, or Cairn.

hooked crosses and trefoils (Figs. 8–9). These emblems, whose significance is not known, are found used as sacred tokens ("religious symbols") among all Indo-European peoples.

c. The iron age begins probably sometime in the fourth century B.C. In very ancient times, even, the Northmen had enjoyed commercial relations with Asia and Greece. From about the time of Christ's birth there begins a strong Roman influence, which, among other things, gives the Gothic-Germanic people a peculiar alphabetic writing, the Runes. The iron age stretches even into historic times; the last division is the Viking time (c. 800–1000). In the course of the iron age people again stopped burning bodies, since, as Snorri says, the cremation-age was succeeded by the mound-age. Bodies were once more regularly provided with objects for use—weapons and vessels for food and drink. Discovery has been made of large and splendid offerings (*e.g.* golden horns), urns with slain animals, perhaps even altars upon which rude images[1] of the gods seem to have been raised (Fig. 10). Several other things from the middle-iron-age will be touched upon in what follows; but we do not see anything really definite, indicating belief in gods, until far on toward Viking times.

---

[1] In a single instance undoubted images of gods were found in certain marshlands.

3. *Common Norse Language.*—At the beginning of the Christian era, the Danes, Norwegians, and Swedes constituted but one tribe, speaking the same language, *Urnordisk*, Primitive Norse. This common language was preserved, with a succession of natural transitions and changes, to be sure, to about the year 1000. In Viking times this was called *den danske Tunge,* "the

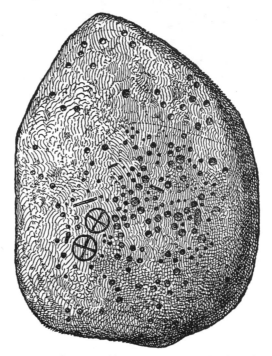

Fig. 4.—Stone with Saucer-like Depressions, Wheels and Crosses.

Danish Tongue," and from it the separate Norse languages have gradually been developed. It is also probable that the Northmen had the same heathen religion in all the main points; even in the worship of the gods there has been but little difference in the different provinces.

Gothic-Germanic Race.—We may even go a step farther back, for it can be established in many ways that Northmen, Germans, and Englishmen also were once one great race, which is usually called the Gothic-Germanic, and this Gothic-Germanic race has again a common origin with most of the

Fig. 5.—Oak Coffins from the Bronze Age.

European peoples (*e.g.* the Greeks), and with the inhabitants of Persia and India.

Indo-Europeans.—We must then picture to ourselves a "primitive people" whose original place of abode we cannot determine, but from which these related peoples have through long periods been developed. This primitive people as a matter of course had certain religious ideas, and it is probable that we may be able to find traces of the original divine faith in the Indian, Greek, and Norse mythology; and this is actually the case. The linguists who are occupied with comparisons between the languages of the different Indo-European races have been able to establish many such points, but here we must be content with bringing forward a few examples.

Aesir.—The general name for the gods was, among the Northmen, *Aesir,* which is developed from the older *Anser.* Corresponding forms are found in most of the related languages.

Fig. 6.—Grave Mound with Urns.

The Heaven-God was called among the Indians *Dyâus,* by the
Greeks *Zeus,* by the Romans *Ju-piter.* The Germanic people
believed in a god whom they called *Tiu,* while there is found in
the Norse religion the name *Tyr* (preserved in Dan. Tirsdag,
Eng. Tuesday). In the oldest Norse language this word must
have been T i w a R.[1] But all these names undoubtedly spring
from a common basal form, which signifies "the bright one" or
"the shining one," and which consequently may have designated the god of the heaven or the sun.

Tyr, Odin, Thor.—Gradually, as the Indo-Europeans scat-
tered and in the course of time settled in different regions with
greatly differing climate, they gave to their god of heaven many
epithets, according to the nature of the country in which they
had settled. The Gothic-Germanic people called him now by
the original name, now WothanaR or ThonaraR ("the blowing
one," "the thundering one"), and it was not long before they forgot that these names were only appendages to the old heaven-
god's name. Now they enumerated as many gods as there were
names, and thus arose, among other things, belief in the three
divinities, Tyr, Odin, and Thor. (The Germans said Wodan and
Donar. In the North we have little or nothing of the worship of
Tyr; Frey takes the place of this god.) Consequently new divinities and new religious ideas seem to have arisen among our forefathers according to the rule that *the god's epithet or title is sep-
arated from his name and then designates an independent*

Fig. 7.—Row of Grave Mounds.

---

[1]*R* answers to voiced *S* in older stages of the language.

personal being. Since this is applicable to a god, one can easily imagine that something similar can be the case with many other points in mythology.

Fig. 8.—Quatrefoil or Hooked Cross.

Fig. 9.—Trefoil

Common Myths.—But a direct comparison also between the heathen faiths of the Indo-European people shows that many single points in their religions (myths) correspond. Myths about a *world-tree* are found among both Indians and Northmen. The

Fig. 10.—Altar from the Iron Age.

highest god among the Indians, Greeks, and our forefathers alike is armed with a sure-striking missile in his capacity of the thunder-god, whether this be represented plainly as a thunder-bolt (lightning-flash), a hammer, or a club.

Cæsar and Tacitus.—Besides this we know but little with certainty about particular points in the mythology of the oldest Gothic-Germanic people; and so it is also with regard to the religion of the Northern people in the first centuries of the Christian era, for they have left no written records behind them. We have already spoken of what we can learn from ancient finds. About the Teutons, taken as a whole, the Roman historians Cæsar and Tacitus give not a few important points of information, especially the latter in his historical books and in his brief account of Germany.

4. *Runes.*—But about the third century after Christ the

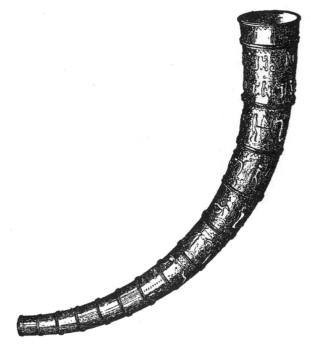

Fig. 11.—A Gold Horn.

Gothic-Germanic people learned to use an alphabet remodeled from the Latin, the so-called "Runes." The Runes soon reached also the Northern races, where they were scratched upon objects in common use, as combs, clasps, weapons, and drinking or sacrificial horns. Here belong the aforementioned golden horns from Gallehus in southern Jutland. These were found in 1639 and 1734 and had a value in our money of about 17,000 kroner ($4,760). At the very beginning of our century they were stolen on account of their great value and melted over, so we now must content ourselves with drawings and casts of these splendid monuments of antiquity, which may have been a sacrificial gift. They consisted of two smooth golden horns of very fine gold with an outer casing of tight-fitting rings likewise of gold, on which there were engraved figures and ornaments, and between these again there were raised figures firmly soldered (Figs. 11–13). Many attempts have been made to interpret these pictorial representations, which easily have a religious significance. Worsaae, our renowned archæologist, was of the opinion that one horn represented life in hell (the serpents), the other life in Valhalla (the stars), which however is wholly uncertain. Along the uppermost ring of one horn one may read in the primitive Norse language:

ek hlewagastiʀ holtingaʀ horna tawido,

that is: I, Lægæst, Holt's son (or, from Holt), made the horn.

Rune-Stones.—Somewhat later men began to use runes for inscriptions on bowlders, which were placed in or oftenest upon grave mounds or elsewhere, as memorials for the departed. Such rune-stones are found in Denmark, Norway, and Sweden from different ages, but with us Danes only from epochs between 800 and 1070,[1] the oldest therefore even from the heathen time. *Rune-stones give the earliest and surest contribution to our knowledge of Aesir-faith in the North.*

Thor on Rune-stones.—On the Glavendrup stone from about

---

[1] Some younger stones from Bornholm and a single one from Skaane need not be mentioned here.

Fig. 12.—Pictures on Gold Horns.

Fig. 13.—Pictures on Gold Horns.

900, which contains the longest Danish runic inscription, we read, after the memorial words themselves, the following:

May Thor consecrate these runes!

On another Danish rune-stone the invocation comprises the whole memorial, for on the margin of the stone is engraved:

May Thor consecrate this monument!

Such a place consecrated or dedicated to the gods is called a *Ve* or *Vi*, which name we have preserved in Odense (*i.e.* Odinsve) and Viborg. On the Glavendrup stone, which is raised over the Chieftain Alle, the latter is called "Vierne's honorable servant," and on a south Jutland rune-stone Chieftain Odinkar's daughter calls herself Vi-Asfrid.

Thor the Chief God.—Only on these two stones is the name of the god of thunder expressly given, but on others we find engraved trefoils, quatrefoils ("hooked crosses"), or hammers (Fig. 14), which is an evidence of the fact that *Thor at this time was the chief god of the Danes;* and this same thing we can establish in many other ways, and for the rest of the North also. This is shown by the many compound person and place names in which Thor's name is the first member (*e.g.* Thorsteinn, Thorbergr). Finally, it can be emphasized that when the Gothic-Germanic people translated the Latin names for the days of the week, in the fifth day, which in Latin is called Jupiter's day (*dies Jovis*), they translated Jupiter by *Thor* (Icel. *Thorsdagr,* Dan. *Torsdag,* Ger. *Donnerstag*).

Odin and Frey.—Together with Thor, Odin and Frey were especially worshiped, and some evidences of this fact are found upon rune-stones. Odin, however, was not understood as the mighty supreme god among the common people. He is so represented only in Norwegian Icelandic poetry, and it was among the Germanic people dwelling southward that Odin-worship played an important part at an early period.

5. *Iceland.*—There are, therefore, but few details known to us of our forefathers' religion at the beginning of Viking times. But from about the year 900 and later we have full and rich information about the religious ideas of the Northern people in the Norwegian-Icelandic literature.

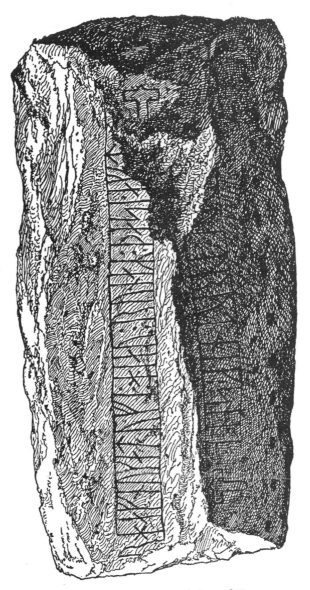

Fig. 14.—Laeborg Stone with Sign of Hammer.

Mythological Poetry.—When different families of the Norwegian nobility at the close of the 9th century began to settle in Iceland, they carried with them from the mother country not only their old religion but also a store of songs and traditions about the gods and heroes. This poetry was preserved faithfully by oral transmission, from generation to generation. Poetical activity soon evinced itself among the Icelanders themselves, and gradually a great and rich literature developed, which became far more important and more truly presented original and national ideas than that of the rest of the Scandinavian country, whose intellectual productions took on through Christianity a foreign, learned-Latin stamp. We can, therefore, expect to find among the Icelanders fuller information about the old faith than elsewhere, and such is also the case. In the Norwegian-Old Icelandic poetry the Norse religion is worked together into a whole, which comprises the creation of the world, the relation of gods to men in life and death, and finally the downfall of the gods and of the world at Ragnarok, after which there shall come a new heaven and a new earth where men are judged after their uprightness and good conduct, and not for their bravery alone.

Odin Chief God.—An essential point which we ought to note here is, as touched upon before, that *Odin in this poetry is conceived of as the chief god,* before whom the others, both gods and goddesses, must bow.

If we now, in what follows, wish to make a coherent presentation of the religion as we find it in Norwegian-Icelandic literature, we must in the first place remember well that Denmark and Sweden hardly had the same faith, viewed as a whole, even if there are points of conformity in essentials. It appears among other things from the myths of the gods which Saxo has presented to us in the first books of his Latin history of Denmark, that various details in the teachings about the gods are told otherwise here (in Denmark) than in Iceland, and that we have traditions to which nothing in Iceland corresponds and vice versa. But in the next place the contention is made, especially by the Norwegian philologist Bugge, that a great many things in mythological poetry, through contact with the Celts and others in the Viking expeditions, have been strongly influenced by Christianity, yes, even by Jewish and Græco-Roman ideas. Against this view, however, many and important objections are raised; but no one can deny that Christianity can and must have had in any case *some* influence upon the later development of Norse mythology. Finally, it cannot be strongly enough emphasized that most of the myths and hero-sagas which are retold in what follows must not be understood as *direct* testimony concerning our fathers' belief, but generally are only a poetically interpreted and modified portrayal, the material for which is most certainly derived from the belief of the people.

Therefore it is Norwegian-Icelandic mythology such as developed in Viking times and soon afterwards (800–1100) which we know best, and it is all we know connectedly. We must see first, then, from what sources we derive this knowledge.

6. *Eddic Poems and Scaldic Lays.*—The oldest and most important sources are the old Norwegian-Icelandic poems. It is customary to distinguish between the so-called Eddic Poems and the Scaldic Lays.

The *Eddic Poems* preserved in an Icelandic manuscript and wrongly called the Elder Edda were composed in the aforementioned period, in the time of transition and of conflict between paganism and Christianity. They are of unknown authorship and treat partly doctrines of the gods and the heathen view of life in connected form, and partly the different sagas of gods and heroes which in the North are usually given a mythological background. The most important of the Eddic poems will be mentioned in the following pages.

The *Scaldic Lays* come from authors whose names are mentioned. The oldest and best are from the same period as the Eddic Poems, but only a few of them have a thoroughly mythological content—chiefly the "shield poems," treating the myths which are pictorially represented on the fields of the shields, and the "Song of Praise" to the chieftain whose lineage is traced up to the gods. On the other hand they all contain in their poetic paraphrases, the so-called *Kenningar,* allusions to mythology or legendary history which presupposes that the myth or saga in question is known to the hearer. When the gallows can be called by a poet "the cool, windy steed of Signy's bridegroom," the hearer must in order to understand the expression know well the legend of Hagbarth and Signy and Hagbarth's death on the gallows. From Iceland came likewise two important primary sources of Norse mythology in prose, namely Snorri's Edda and the Saga of the Volsungs.

7. *Snorri (d. 1241)*.—Snorri Sturlason was Iceland's most important prose author and withal a clever Scald. In his historical masterpiece, "Heimskringla," he used especially for matters concerning the earliest time, old Scaldic lays as proofs for his description, and therefore he acquired accurate and intimate knowledge of their content: and as a Scald he of necessity completely understood the substance and nature of the poetical paraphrases. He then conceived the plan of committing his knowledge to writing, and therefore he composed his Edda. This word is most closely defined as "Poetics" or "Handbook for Scalds." The book falls into three main divisions. The first, *Gylfaginning*, 'Delusion of Gylfi,' relates the story of a king Gylfi, who journeyed forth to learn about the power of the Aesir. He disguised himself as a wayfarer and came to a great hall in which were many people and three chieftains, who sat each in his high seat, one higher than the other. These he questioned about all the mythological relations, and he received clear answers to all his inquiries. Within this framework Snorri takes occasion to present a general view of the whole doctrine of the gods, particularly following old poems which he frequently cites in evidence. He mentions several of the Eddic poems still preserved, but also some which we do not know now from any other source.

The second section, *Skaldskaparmal*,[1] reviews and explains the different poetic paraphrases. Where these allude to the doctrine of the gods or to traditional history, the myths or traditions in question are recounted and a number of scaldic verses are cited as passages in evidence.

The third section, finally, *Hattatal*,[2] which is the least important for the mythology, is a practical application of the foregoing

---

[1]Poetic Phraseology or Language of Poetry.
[2]Enumeration or Tale of Meters.

theory, since Snorri has composed a number of verses in different meters, making use of the paraphrases which he has explained in what preceded.

In the introduction to the whole and in the arrangement of the material one easily feels that Snorri has sought to bring about coherence in the old traditions—perhaps involuntarily under influence of his Christian faith—and tries to coin history out of myths and sagas, since Odin is made into a prince versed in magic, dwelling originally in Asia, but who later wandered to the North, where he became the ancestor of the kings of the realm and was worshiped as a god. Snorri advances the same view also in the first part of the Heimskringla,[1] the so-called Ynglinga Saga, which contains important but obscure mythological information.

The Saga of the Volsungs contains a connected prose version of the Sagas of the Volsungs and Nibelung, an amplified renarration of the Eddic Hero-Poems; but here, as in Gylfaginning, it is apparent that the unknown author had for his authority poems now lost.

But in the other pieces of Icelandic prose literature also there are given here and there important details about the heathen worship of the gods and its forms. This applies both to the Heimskringla (the attempt of the two Olafs to introduce Christianity into Norway) and to not a few of the family-sagas. There are also found mythical-heroic sagas in the style of the Volsunga Saga and romantic sagas with mythological material.

8. Popular Songs and Saxo.—In the German saga-poetry Dietrich von Bern (Theodoric of Verona) plays the leading part, and tales about him have also wandered to the North, where they are treated both in Eddic poetry and in folk-songs. Meanwhile the same theme is treated far more explicitly in the Thithrek Saga, which was composed in Norway in the middle of the 13th century on the basis of tales and songs of Low German merchants.

Folk-Songs.—Finally, an important but late source is found in the ancient ballads proper, which partly contain allusions to

---

[1] "The Round World," History of the Scandinavian Races.

myths ("Tor of Havsgaard," "The Youth Svejdal," "Sven Vonved," "Aage and Else"), and partly treat whole saga-cycles ("The Volsungs," "Hagbarth and Signe"). In several of the magic songs also there are preserved many heathen ideas, while their apparent Christian character is somewhat superficial. Here we can also mention *popular traditions* and *popular adventures* and especially *popular usages*, which have often preserved one or another heathen reminiscence.

As already remarked above, Saxo in his ancient history, the first nine books of his works, retells and works in together a number of sagas about the gods, heroes, and kings. In his work, which was finished in the beginning of the 13th century, he has made use of both Danish and Icelandic tradition for its foundation. The ancient history has extraordinary mythological importance, but as a source it must be used with the greatest caution. Saxo gives the same historical interpretation to the whole that he does to any part and therefore he has altered and rearranged myths and sagas when coherence seemed to demand it. The old gods are interpreted as might be expected from a religious author. Old songs are often quoted, but unfortunately in a remodeled Latin version.

NOTE.—Canon Adam of Bremen, who lived contemporaneously with Svend Estridson, made a Latin account of the history of the Archbishop of Hamburg, in which he also tells of the paganism of the Northern countries. Of foreign sources which can throw light upon the interrelation of myths among the Gothic-Germanic people can be named the "History of the Goths," written by Jordanes, and the "History of the Lombards," by Paulus Diaconus. Finally, there are found important contributions on this point in Old German and Anglo-Saxon poetry, which is now purely heathen, now Christian with a background of heathen ideas and expressions. In England are found not a few pictorial representations with half-heathen content, of which several will be used in what follows.

FIRST SECTION

I. How the World Was Created

1. THE FOG-COUNTRY AND THE FIRE-WORLD.—Long years before the earth existed, *Niflheim* was created. In the midst of it lay the well *Hvergelmir,* from which ten ice-cold venomous streams, *Elivagar,* had their origin. Niflheim lay toward the north, but southward there was a place called *Muspell,* where it was light and hot, glowing and burning, and therefore impassable for any one who had not his home there. At Muspell's boundary sat *Surt* as defender of the country, with a flaming sword in his hand; it was he who at the destruction of the world was to lead in the battle against the gods and set the earth on fire. Midway between the fog-country and the fire-world there was a yawning gulf, *Ginnungagap.*

2. THE PRIMITIVE GIANT YMIR.—The waves of the venomous streams soon froze to ice and the poisonous vapor condensed to frost, which was met by the warm air from Muspell. From this contact came into being the primitive giant *Ymir,* and he became the ancestor of the race of giants, as both heaven and earth also were afterward constructed from his body. Once when he was asleep he fell into a perspiration and from under his left arm came forth a man and a woman; but it was even more wonderful that one of his feet begot a son with the other. This son again had a son by name *Bergelmir.*

The Cow Authumla; Bor's Sons.—The congealed venomous streams continued to send out frost, and from this the cow *Authumla* stood forth. From her udders there came four streams of milk, from which Ymir got his nourishment, while the

21

cow herself lived by licking the salt, frost-covered stones. On the first day she licked them there came forth toward evening a man's hair, the next day a man's head, and the third day the whole man stood there. He was named *Buri*, and was fair, tall, and mighty to look upon. Later he had a son by name *Bor*, who married the giant *Bolthorn's* daughter *Bestla*. Their sons were *Odin, Vili,* and *Ve.*

The whole story of the creation is told explicitly in Snorri's "Edda," but is mentioned also in the beginning of the old poem, *Voluspa*, the Volva's Prophecy:

VSP. 3

'Twas the beginning of time   when Ymir lived,
there was no sand nor sea   nor billows cool;
earth was found nowhere   neither heaven above;
a gulf was Ginnunga   but grass was nowhere.

3. HEAVEN AND EARTH.—Bor's sons now took Ymir and killed him. So much blood flowed from his wound that all his progeny was drowned in it, with the exception of his son's son Bergelmir and his wife, who saved themselves from the streams of blood in a boat or tree-trunk, and later became the ancestors of a new race of giants. But Bor's sons took the giant's body, brought it out into the midst of the yawning gulf, and formed heaven and earth from it.

In one of the Eddic poems we get more exact information as to how this came to pass:

GRIMN. 40

From Ymir's flesh   the earth was shaped
and from his blood the sea,
the mountains from his bones   trees from his hair,
and from his skull the sky.

41

And from his eye-lashes   the kindly gods made
Mithgarth for the sons of men,
and from his brain   were the forbidding
clouds all shaped.

The heaven was made fast over the earth by four corners;

under each of these sat a dwarf who bore the same name as the corner of the earth. The sparks that went out from Muspell, the sons of Bor placed everywhere in the sky over the yawning gulf, so that they should illuminate the world. Now it was the sun, moon, and stars which had their places and courses appointed for men's computation of time, while the lightning went freely around. The earth was spherical in form, and out around it flowed the great sea, along whose coast the giants obtained land for settlement—*Jotunheim,* 'Giants' Home.' But midway between, Odin and his brothers constructed Mithgarth, hedged about with the primitive giant's eyelashes; there, men were to have their dwelling-place.

REMARK.—Terms like Mithgarth, applied to the world of men, appear among the Goths, Anglo-Saxons, and Germans. In a Danish ballad our dead Lord begs leave to return to *Middelhjem.*

4. DAY AND NIGHT.—In Jotunheim there dwelt meanwhile a man who was named *Nor,* and who had a daughter by the name of *Nat.* She was dark and swarthy, like all her family. Nat was married to *Delling,* of Bor's race, and with him she had a son, *Dag,* who was light and handsome like his father. Odin now took mother and son and set them up in heaven, over which they were to drive every twenty-four hours.

Nat drives first with the steed *Hrimfaxi,* from whose bit foam flies down over the earth; this is what we call dew. Following after comes Dag with his steed *Skinfaxi,* whose mane throws radiance over air and land.

5. SUN AND MOON.—A man, by name *Mundilfari,* had two children, who were so fair that he called the son *Mani* and the daughter *Sol.* But the gods were offended at his arrogance and placed both the children up in heaven, where they have to drive the cars of the moon and sun. The sun steeds were called *Arvak* and *Alsvith,* 'perfectly wise'; under their bellies were two pairs of bellows to cool them. Mani guides the course of the moon and controls its increase and its waning.

The reason that Sol and Mani pass so hurriedly over is that they are pursued by wolves. Their mother is a giantess, who dwells in the forest *Jarnvith,* east of Mithgarth. The moon-wolf is also called *Managarm*. He is satisfied with flesh of dead men, and is to redden the seat of the gods with blood when he swallows the moon; but this will not happen before the destruction of the world.

The places and courses of the heavenly bodies determine chronology and the divisions of the year. Of seasons, only two are named. The father of Winter is called *Vindsval*, but Summer is a son of *Svasuth*, 'the mild.'

6. WIND AND RAINBOW.—*Hraesvelg*, 'body-destroyer,' is a giant in eagle's form, who sits toward the north at the end of heaven and with the blustering strokes of his wings sends out gales over land and people without the wind itself ever being seen.

Between heaven and earth goes the tri-colored bridge the rainbow which is called *Bif-rost* or *Asebro*. Over this ride the gods to their place of assembly in heaven—with the exception of Thor, who takes a shorter route by fording the streams beneath it. If he should drive over with his wagon, Asebro would break and take fire; but this shall not happen until Ragnarok, when Surt rides over it at the head of Muspell's sons. At the end of the bridge up in the mountains of heaven dwells *Heimdall*, who guards the bridge against the mountain giants.

7. DWARFS AND ELVES.—In addition to giants and gods, there were also created other living beings, among them dwarfs and elves.

Dwarfs were small, ugly creatures, but possessed great sagacity and skill. Some of them dwelt in stones, others in the earth. According to the Eddic Poems, they were created from the blood and bones of two giants whom the gods had slain, while Snorri relates that they had come into existence like maggots in the flesh of the slaughtered Ymir. Nothing distinct is told of the creation of the *Elves*. They were kindly disposed toward gods and men, and so were called light elves, but in Snorri dark elves are also mentioned, who soon came to be regarded as evil spirits.

8. THE WORLD-TREE AND THE NORNS.—In the midst of the world stood a great tree, the ash *Ygg-drasil* (Odin's house, *i.e.* Odin's gallows), at the foot of which the gods had their place of

assembly. This ash is the largest and best of all trees: the branches spread themselves over the whole world and rise high up over
heaven. The tree has three main roots.
In an Eddic Poem it is said of these:

GRIMN. 3
Three roots stretch out   in three directions
under the ash of Ygg-drasil:
Hel lives under one,   under the second the frost-giants,
under the third the race of men.

Snorri relates that one root stands among the Aesir, the second among the frost-giants, and the third over Niflheim. Under
the last root, upon which the dragon *Nithhogg* gnaws, the well
Hvergelmir is found. Under the root among the frost-giants lies
Mimir's well, in which all wisdom and understanding are concealed. It is owned by the giant *Mimir,* who dips his drink from
it every morning with the *Gjallarhorn.* Odin had to pledge one
of his eyes to him for a single draught from the well of wisdom.
Under the world-tree's third root there is a very sacred spring,
which is called *Urth's Well.* Here is the gods' assembly place,
where they deliberate every day and hold their court. By the
well there is a splendid hall, in which the *Norns* or Fates have
their dwelling. These deliberate about destinies in the world. In
the later Icelandic sources three are named: *Urth, Verthandi,*
and *Skuld,* but at times many more are mentioned, now of the
race of gods and now of the race of elves.
   The Norns sprinkle the world-tree every day with water from
Urth's well, that it may thrive and continue fresh. In the well two
swans are nurtured, and from them the swans of the earth proceed. The water in the well is so pure that everything which is
moistened in it becomes completely white.
   Of the ash-tree there is still to be told that in its branches lives
a very clever eagle, between whose eyes sits a hawk. Up and
down among the branches darts a squirrel, *Ratatosk,* and carries
hateful words between the eagle and Nithhogg. Again, four deer
run between the branches and eat the leaves of the tree, and in
Hvergelmir there are so many serpents that no one can count
them.

9. MEN ARE CREATED.—It chanced one time that the sons of Bor were walking along the beach, where they found two trees. They pulled them up by the roots and fashioned two human beings from them, a man and a woman. The first of the sons gave them soul and life; the second, understanding and the power of motion; the third, visage, speech, hearing, and sight. After that they gave them clothing and names. The man they called *Ask* and the woman *Embla,* and from them descend all the inhabitants of Mithgarth, and therefore the whole human race. In some verses inserted in the Volva's Prophecy, in which the creation of man is narrated, the three gods are called *Odin, Hœnir* and *Lothur,* while the sons of Bor are in every other case named Odin, Vili and Ve. The gods now built for themselves in the midst of the world a castle, which they called *Asgarth.* Odin married Frigg, and from them descend the gods or the race of Aesir. With Jorth, Odin had a son, Thor.

Fig. 15.—Cross and Ash Tree.

REMARK.—The belief in sacred trees at whose root springs rise and where wise women have their dwelling is very ancient and is often mentioned among the Gothic-Germanic people. Bugge is of the opinion that the doctrine of the world-tree is influenced by the idea of the Christian Cross; this is represented, *e.g.* on English stone-crosses from the earliest Christian times in a form which reminds one of Yggdrasil (Fig. 15). It is possible, but far from certain, that Bugge is right, since the opposite view is just as plausible.

II. The Gods and Their Life

1. THE GOLDEN AGE.—After an account has been given in the Volva's Prophecy of the conditions at the beginning of time, the poem continues:

VSP. 4

Early the sons of Bor   earth's surface raised,
they who Mithgarth   the wondrous shaped.
The sun shone from the south   on the stones of the ground
then was earth grown   with green herbs.

7

The Aesir met   on Ida-field,
who sanctuary and temple   erected high;
forges they placed   rich treasures wrought;
tongs they shaped   and tools they made.

8

They played at draughts   in court, were joyful,
they in no wise had   a lack of gold—
until three came,   the giant maids,
of greatest might,   from Jotunheim.

The Golden Age of the gods, time of innocence, did not last very long. As a warning that "sin was to come into the world," the three giant maidens appeared, commonly supposed to be the Norns. This feature reappears in the most developed heathen religions; one cannot comprehend the relation of things in the world without assuming a belief in inexorable fate, to which even the gods themselves must bow. The heathen gods are mighty, but not almighty.

2. THE VANIR.—Besides the gods who descend from Bor, the Northern people have also conceived of another race of gods, the *Vanir,* as to whose origin the old sources give us few and obscure particulars. Only one thing can be definitely stated: it came to a conflict between the two races of gods. This ended, as it seems, in a victory for the Aesir, after which the contending parties concluded peace and reconciliation and gave each other hostages. By this means *Njorth* and his two children, *Frey* and *Freyja,* came to Asgarth.

REMARK.—In the Ynglinga Saga, Snorri gives closer information: the Vanir who lived in Vanaheim gave as a hostage their most excellent man, Njorth the Rich, and his son Frey, but the Aesir in return gave Hœnir, who in every respect looked as a chieftain ought and who was a tall and very handsome man. With him the Aesir sent the very wise Mimir, and the Vanir gave for him the wisest man in their number, *Kvasir.* Hœnir became forthwith a noted chieftain, for *Mimir* gave him advice against all dangers. But if he was admitted to the court or in other assemblies where Mimir was not present, and when one or another difficult matter was laid before him, he always answered: "Let others decide it." So the Vanir soon conceived a suspicion that the Aesir had duped them in the exchange of hostages, wherefore they took Mimir, beheaded him, and sent his head to the Aesir. Odin anointed the head with medicinal herbs, so that it could not decay, and pronounced magic songs over it, so that it spoke and revealed to him many secret matters.

The Vanir were versed in magic to a peculiar degree. Freyja was the first who practiced enchantments among the Aesir, a kind of magic prevalent among the Vanir. Njorth was the father of the two children mentioned in union with his sister; but among the Aesir, marriage between such near relatives was forbidden.

The Volva's Prophecy relates that the occasion for the conflict was this. There came a woman versed in magic, by name *Gollveig,* from the Vanir to Asgarth. She caused nothing but calamities, and the Aesir resolved to slay her. They raised her on a spear and burned her upon a pyre, but she was born again three times and burned anew. The Vanir claimed redress, but no agreement was reached:

VSP. 24
Odin hurled   and shot against the warriors;
that was the war,   the first in the world;
shattered was the wall   of the castle of the gods,
the warlike Vanir could   tread the field.

We ourselves can now draw the inference that the Aesir had to conclude peace; the poem tells nothing of this, nor does it tell how the gods got their castle rebuilt.

Snorri says that they contracted with a giant builder for this work; he was allowed to have the help only of his horse *Svathilfari,* and was to complete the work in one winter. If the castle was finished on the first day of summer, he should have Freyja and the sun and moon as reward for his building. The Aesir made these terms upon Loki's advice, and the giant made the gods take solemn oath that they would give him free conduct. The work advanced rapidly, and when it neared completion the Aesir were provoked with Loki and wanted to slay him if he did not contrive a remedy. Loki grew anxious for his life, and perceived that all depended upon depriving the giant of his assistant, the horse. He therefore transformed himself into a mare, which enticed Svathilfari into the woods away from the work. When the builder saw that his undertaking could not be accomplished at the right time, he became furious; so the gods had to call upon Thor. "He soon was there, and then the hammer Mjolnir flew into the air: he[1] became the one, not Sol and Mani, who paid the reward for the work. The first blow was such that his skull burst into small pieces." Of the mare was afterward born a foal, which became Odin's renowned steed, the eight-footed *Sleipnir.*

While Snorri obviously delights in Thor and the strength with which he crushes the poor giant, in the Volva's Prophecy there is seriousness and alarm in the portrayal: for the gods have committed murder, and now there comes a new state of affairs, which is introduced with treachery and infidelity:

VSP. 26
Thor alone fought there,   filled with wrath;
he seldom sits   when he learns such things.

---

[1]The builder.

Broken were oaths   and words and vows,
all solemn pacts   between them made.

Odin is disquieted at this, since he foresees that the happiness
of the gods now is past, and he fears for what is to come. Seized
with foreboding, he has Gjallarhorn concealed at Mimir's well,
and pledges one of his eyes to the wise giant for a single draught
from the fountain of wisdom.

Here we must pause for a time to give a portrayal of the individual gods and goddesses, with their relation to men.
  3. AESIR AND ASYNJUR.—"Then said Gangleri (*i.e.* King Gylfi):
Which are the Aesir in whom it is man's duty to believe? Har
answers: *Twelve are the Aesir of the race of gods.* Then said
Jafnhar: *The Asynjur are not less holy and they are not less capable.* Then said Thrithi: *Odin is the greatest and oldest of the
Aesir.*"
  We have been told before how Snorri has brought a certain
system into the teaching about the gods. He particularly attach-
es great value to the introduction of the numbers three and
twelve into his presentation. Although there were doubtless
very few of these gods and goddesses whom our forefathers
really worshiped, they are so often met in later poetry that we
must begin with a short account of them all, following Snorri as
closely as possible.
  4. ODIN is the greatest and oldest of the Aesir, and governs all
things; however mighty the other gods are, they all serve him as
children their father. *Frigg* is his wife, and she knows exactly the
fate of every man, but yet does not occupy herself with divina-
tion. Odin is called "All-father," because he is father of all the
gods, but is called also "Valfathir," because all those are his chosen sons who fall on the field of battle. He gives them places in
Valhalla and *Vingolf,* and there they are called *Einherjar.* Odin
is also called God of the Hanged, and has many more names,
which can be read in the Eddic Poem *Grimnismal.*
  5. THOR is foremost among the other Aesir: he is called *Asa-
Thor* and *Aka-Thor,* and is the strongest of all gods and men. His
kingdom is called *Thruthheim* or *Thruthvangar,* but his abode is

called *Bilskirnir*. In the hall there are five hundred and forty rooms, and it is the largest house that was ever built. Thor has two goats; when he drives, they draw his wagon, and he is called *Aka-Thor*. He has besides three wonderful treasures: one is the hammer *Mjolnir*, which the frost giants and mountain giants recognize when he comes—and that is not so strange, either, for it has crushed many a skull of their fathers and kinsmen; next, the strength-girdle—when he puts it about him, his godlike strength grows twofold; finally, the iron mittens for grasping the hammershaft. No one is so well versed in knowledge of the past that he can recount all of Thor's mighty deeds.

6. Another son of Odin is BALDUR. Of him there is only good to tell; he is the best of all and all praise him. He is so fair and shining in visage that light comes from him, and there is a plant so white that it has been compared to the god's eyelashes and called "Baldur's brow"; it is the whitest of all plants. Baldur is the wisest, most eloquent and gracious of all the Aesir. This peculiarity follows him, however, that none of his decisions hold. His dwelling is in heaven in *Breithablik,* and in this place there can be nothing impure.

7. NJORTH dwells in heaven in *Noatun*. He governs the course of the wind and calms the sea and fire; to him shall men call, upon the sea and in the chase. He is so rich in land and gods that he can give richly of these to those who ask. He was really born in Vanaheim, but as we have heard before, the Vanir gave him as a hostage to the gods in Asgarth. He was married to *Skathi,* a daughter of a giant, *Thiazzi.* Skathi much preferred to live up in *Thrymheim,* among the mountains, where her father had his farm. Njorth, on the contrary, was most attached to the vicinity of the sea. So they agreed to stay alternately, nine days in Thrymheim and then nine in Noatun; but when Njorth came back from the mountains he said: Odious to me are the mountains, and yet I tarried there not long, only nine nights; and the howling of the wolves methinks is evil compared with the singing of the swans. But Skathi answered about Noatun: I could not sleep on the borders of the shore for the screaming of the birds; every morning the gull wakens me when it comes from the sea. After that she moved up into the mountains and

continued to dwell there. She often runs upon snowshoes and shoots deer with her bow, wherefore she is also called the "Snowshoe Goddess."

8. FREY AND FREYJA.—Njorth of Noatun, as we have said, had had two children in Vanaheim, a son, Frey, and a daughter, Freyja. Frey is the grandest among the Aesir: he governs the rain and sunshine and thereby the products of the earth; wherefore men shall call upon him to obtain good years and times of peace, as he also governs men's happiness with reference to the gods. His dwelling is called *Alfheim*. His sister, Freyja, is the most excellent among the Asynjur, and dwells in heaven in the castle which is called *Folkvang*. When she rides to battle she takes half the *Val*, 'the slain,' but Odin the other half. Her hall is called *Sessrymnir*, and she has a wagon drawn by two cats. One is to call upon her in everything which concerns love. She herself had as husband a man named *Od*, whom she dearly loved, but he forsook her and set out on a long journey, while she remained behind weeping. Her tears were red gold; she owned the costly ornament *Brisingamen*, wherefore she is called *Menglath*, 'glad in adornment.' Of her other epithets, *Gefn*, *Vanadis*, and *Mardal*, 'the one shining over the sea' may be emphasized.

9. TYR is the most hardy and courageous among the Aesir. He is master especially of victory in combat, and for this reason brave men should call upon him. As a proof of his bravery, the chaining of the Fenris Wolf (§14) can be cited, in which he lost his right hand. Tyr is therefore called the one-handed god, but no one calls him the reconciler of men.

10. BRAGI is god of the scaldic art, and he is married to ITHUN, who guards the apples which the gods eat when they grow old. Afterwards they grow young again, and so it will continue until Ragnarok.

11. HEIMDALL is called the white god; he is great and holy. Nine maids, all sisters, bore him. He is also called *Gullintanni*, for his teeth are of gold, and his horse is called *Gulltop*. As mentioned above, he dwells in the mountains of heaven at the end of the bridge of the Aesir, as caretaker of the bridge and of the gods. He needs less sleep than a bird, sees a hundred *rasts*

(miles) before him just as well by night as by day, and has such acute hearing that he hears the grass growing in the field and the wool upon the sheep. His horn is called *Gjallarhorn* (Fig. 16[1]), which sounds so loud that it can be heard over all worlds, and his sword is called *Hofuth,* 'head.'

12. OTHER AESIR.—We can further mention Odin's blind son, *Hothr,* the silent god; *Vithar,* who is next strongest after Thor; *Vali,* son of Odin and *Rind;* and also Thor's stepson, *Ull* of

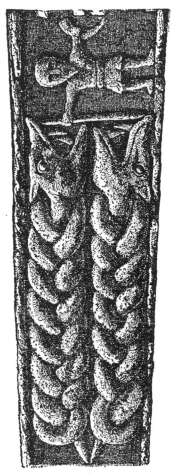

Fig. 16.—Heimdall with Horn.

---

[1]From an English stone cross: Heimdall representing Christ?

Ydalir, who is unrivaled as an archer and snow-skater and good to call upon in single combat. *Forseti* is the name of the son of Baldur and Nanna, daughter of *Nep,* who owns in heaven the hall *Glitnir,* and is the god of justice, who adjusts all difficult matters that arise.

In Helgoland (Fositi's land) a divinity Fositi was worshiped when the Christian missionaries arrived, and he is taken for the same as the Forseti of the Norsemen. He had a great temple; no one was allowed to touch his herd of cattle or other property, and from his sacred well one might draw only in silence.

13. LOKI.—In the number of the Aesir we can also count the one whom some call the gods' occasioner of quarrels, the originator of all fraud and the disgrace of gods and men. He is called *Loki,* or *Lopt,* and is son of the giant *Farbauti* and the giantess *Laufey.* Loki is handsome and fair in countenance but evil in character and of very changeable mien. He is gifted with great ingenuity and cunning, and although he caused the Aesir the greatest misfortunes, he could just as often with his shrewdness invent means of escape from difficulties. Loki's wife was named *Sigyn,* their son *Nari,* or *Narfi.*

14. LOKI'S OFFSPRING.—But Loki had other children. In Jotunheim lived a woman by name *Angrbotha,* and with her Loki had terrible offspring: the wolf *Fenrir,* the serpent *Mithgarthsorm,* and *Hel.* Since it was prophesied that these children should cause great calamities, the gods cast the Mithgarth serpent out into the deep ocean-world, where it grew great and encircled the whole earth. Hel was cast down into Niflheim, where she became queen of the underworld, but the Aesir brought up the wolf at their home. When he grew up his evil nature became fairly known, and therefore they resolved to bind him. The first two chains he burst with ease. Only the third fetter, *Gleipnir,* could hold, and that, to be sure, was made of the noise of a cat's paw, the beard of a woman, the roots of a mountain, the sinews of a bear, the breath of a fish, and the spittle of a bird. The wolf was not willing that the slender and insignificant fetter should be placed upon him, since he suspected fraud, until Tyr put his right hand as a pledge into the monster's

mouth. All the gods laughed when the fetter bound his limbs together, excepting Tyr; he had lost his right hand.

15. THE ASYNJUR.—"Which are the *Asynjur,* 'goddesses'? Har answers, *Frigg is the supreme one.*" She has a very magnificent dwelling, which is called *Fensal.* However, we have told about her and Freyja above. Another goddess is *Saga,* in *Sokkvabek; Ejr* is the best physician; *Gefjon* is a maiden, and she is served by all those who die as maidens; another maiden is *Fulla,* who has streaming hair with a golden head-band,—she is Frigg's handmaid and knows her secret plans. We can further mention *Var,* the goddess of promises, who listens to the agreements which men and women make with each other, while she also avenges every infringement of them; and also *Sjofn* and *Lofn.*

Valkyrs.—Now those women must be named who are called *Valkyrjur* and serve at table in Valhalla. Odin sends them to every battle; they "choose the slain," and have control of the strife and its result. There are many mentioned with different names, all of which mean "battle" and "tumult of war."

16. LIFE IN VALHALLA.—Valhalla is thatched with golden shields and has five hundred and forty doors. Through each of these eight hundred Einherjar can go at one time. Outside of Valhalla lies the grove *Glasir,* whose foliage is shining gold. Odin's heroes live from the flesh which the boar *Saehrimnir* yields them; they drink beside the mead which flows from the udders of the goat *Heithrun,* while the goat feeds on the leaves from Valhalla's tree.

Every day, when the Einherjar awake, they put on their armor and go out upon the court to fight against each other. But the fallen rise again, and all return at evening, joyous and reconciled, to the drinking bout in Odin's hall. Thus it reads in the Eddic Poem of *Vafthruthnir:*

VAFTH. 41

All Einherjar   at Odin's court
contend together every day;
the slain they choose   and ride from the fray;
sit, thereupon in peace together.

But it is only the brave dying in arms who go to Odin; those
dying of disease go down to the shadow realm of Hel.

17. THE WORLD'S DOWNFALL APPROACHES.—In the Volva's
Prophecy the further course of the life of gods and men is
described. We see how correct Odin's evil forebodings were.
The Valkyrs ride away, brandishing their spears, which signifies
trouble and war in the earth. The giants begin to assemble and
equip themselves for the last battle with the gods, and now
comes to pass also the world's greatest misfortune: Baldur, the
god of gentleness and innocence, goes, according to the decree
of fate, to Hel's abode. Evil dreams have augured danger for his
life. Frigg takes oath of everything dead and living, excepting
the slender and supple but beautiful shoot, the Mistletoe:

VSP. 33–34
There grew from the tree   what slender seemed
a perilous pain-shaft;   Hothr did shoot;
But Frigg shed tears   in Fensal
for Valhalla's woe;   do ye yet know? or how?

18. LOKI IS PUNISHED.—Indeed, it is Baldur's blind brother
who becomes the instrument of fate: but behind him stands
Loki, the originator of all evil. The gods inflict terrible punishment upon him, as with his own son's intestines they bind him
fast to three stones set upon edge, and fix a poisonous serpent
over his face. Meanwhile his faithful wife Sigyn stands by him
and catches the poison in a bowl; but every time it is filled and
she must empty its contents, Loki writhes in terrible pain, so
that the earth trembles (Fig. 17[1]). This is really of but little
advantage, since Baldur must remain with Hel. Odin's swain,
Hermoth, gained of the death-goddess permission for Baldur's
return in case *everything* in the world should weep over his
death. It was done; only a giant woman, *Thokk,* whom they
found in a gloomy mountain cavern, would "weep with dry
tears," wherefore Hel kept what she had. But it is commonly

---

[1]From an English stone cross. The picture is commonly understood to represent
Loki's punishment, since Loki is said to signify "the bound devil." Cf. the two fore-
going figures and the remark on Bugge's interpretation. (Introd. "Home of the
Eddic Poems.")

thought that it was Loki who had taken on this giant woman's form in order to set a crown upon his work.

19. NASTROND.—Now evil really breaks loose, and great crimes are committed in the world; perjured men, murderers, and seducers must wade through heavy streams into a hall on *Nastrond,* "death-shore," far from the sun. Its door turns toward the north, poison drips in at the louver, and the ceiling is plaited with serpent's backs. Moral corruption increases in a frightful degree:

Fig. 17.—Loki's Punishment.

VSP. 45
Brothers will fight together   and become each other's bane,
sister's children   will violate kinship;
it is evil in the world,   adultery serious, . . .
no man will   spare another.

Then comes finally the fearful encounter between the warrior gods and the evil powers in the earth, in which all go to destruction. But the conclusion of the conflict means only that a new earth, with gods and men in purified forms, arises.

III. Ragnarok

1. THE ENEMIES OF THE GODS ASSEMBLE.—In the last periods of the world came first the frightful *Fimbulvetr*, 'great winter,' which is repeated three times. When the deciding moment draws near, the world-tree trembles although it still remains standing; all in Hel's kingdom take fright, the dwarfs groan in the mountains, and there is a crashing in Jotunheim, while the gods hold their last assembly and Heimdall sends the calling tones of the Gjallarhorn out over the world. Fenrir bursts his chains, and the Mithgarth serpent writhes in giant wrath and lashes the sea into towering waves. From the east comes *Hrym* with the ship *Naglfar*, built of dead men's nails; from the north sail Hel's sons over the sea, with Loki in command; and Surt rides on from the south, with flaming sword, at the head of Muspell's sons. Then the bridge of the Aesir falls under the horses' hoofs and heaven is on fire. Fenrir goes forth with yawning mouth; his upper jaw touches heaven while his lower jaw drags along the earth. Fire spurts out from the monster's eyes and nostrils when Odin meets him in battle only to be swallowed up by the terrible abyss. Heimdall fights with Loki; Frey and Surt become each other's destroyers.

2. THOR FIGHTS WITH THE MITHGARTH SERPENT.—The last incident in the conflict is Thor's victory over the Mithgarth serpent. The mighty god of heaven and earth crushes with his hammer the head of his deadly foe; but only nine steps does he totter on, before he sinks dead to the earth, choked by the serpent's poison.

VSP. 55

Then comes the great   son of Hlothyn;
there yawns across the air   the Girdle of the earth[1]—
fire it spurts,   poison it spews[2]
Odin's son goes   to meet the worm.

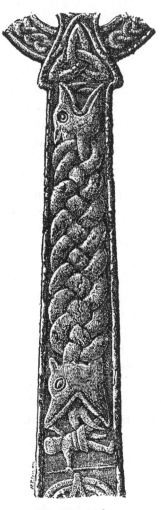

Fig. 18.—Vithar.

---

[1]Mithgarth Serpent.
[2]Not in Sijmon's text.

56

Strikes with wrath   Mithgarth's defender;
all men will   forsake their home.
Nine feet goes   Fjorgyn's son
bowed, from the snake,   who fears no shame.

Now the sun grows dark, the earth sinks into the sea, the clear stars fall from heaven, and everything goes up in fire and flame. This is *Ragna-rok*, the gods' crisis, the last destiny by which the gods of Valhalla are overtaken.

3. SNORRI'S VERSION.—Snorri renarrates the Ragnarok myths with detailed descriptions of all the incidents. The battle was fought on the plain *Vigrith*, which is a hundred rasts on every side. Tyr fights with the Hel hound *Garm*, sun and moon are swallowed by the wolves, and it is Surt who hurls fire over the earth. But within the time, *Vithar*, Odin's silent son, has avenged the death of the Father of the Gods; he steps with his heavy shoe on the wolf's under jaw, grasps with his hands the upper jaw, and afterwards tears the monster's mouth asunder (Fig. 18).[1]

----

4. REGENERATION.—But the downfall is only temporary and not everlasting. The Volva's Prophecy continues with its charming description of the new heaven and earth where justice and peace shall prevail. The earth rises once more, green and glorious, from the sea. The regenerated gods meet again on Idaplain, recall the Mithgarth serpent, the old life of the gods, and the last terrible summons of fate. Then they find in the grass the wonderful golden tablets which they themselves owned in the morning of time. Then dawn a new golden age and a calm period of happiness, which is to be everlasting:

VSP. 62

Unsown will   acres grow,
all evil will be cured,   Baldur will come;
Hoth and Baldur dwell in Hropt's battle-home,[2]
abode of war-gods.   Do ye yet know? or how?

-----

[1]From an English stone cross; cf. Fig. 17.
[2]Valhalla.

64

A hall I know is standing   fairer than the sun,
thatched with gold,   at Gimli;
there shall the faithful   hosts abide
and for lasting time   delights enjoy.

65

There comes the mighty one,   to the sublime tribunal,
strong from above,   who governs all things.

5. THE NEW GENERATION.—Nor does Snorri know how to inform us who the great ruler is. On the contrary he tells, in harmony with another Eddic lay, about the rise of the new race of men. In Hoddmimir's grove two persons, *Lif* and *Lifthrasir*, were hiding during the burning of the world; they received morning dew for nourishment, and from them descend all the future races of men. Through an old song we learn, moreover, that *Alf-rotholl*, 'elf-glance,' *i.e.* the sun, before the wolf swallows her, bears a daughter. The maiden is to drive in her mother's course when the gods are dead.

SECOND SECTION

SOULS, DEMONS, AND GODS

I. Common Popular Belief
(Lower Mythology)

1. LOWER MYTHOLOGY—It has been pointed out in the General Introduction that the worship of souls and nature-demons, the oldest foundation of heathen religion, has yielded a succession of superstitious ideas, which have held very long in the minds of the people and of which we find evident traces even in our day. The same basal ideas reappear among all heathen people, although in details the belief may have developed in a very distinct manner. We find here a marked conformity among all the Gothic-Germanic peoples, and we shall now bring forward some of the chief points from this so-called *lower mythology,* independent of the more developed national religion which in the main acquires its character from those most highly developed in the community.

2. NIGHTMARE.—Our forefathers, like other heathen people, found one of the plainest proofs of the soul's independence of the body and its ability to take a hand in the affairs of living men in the nightmare and dream, as they lacked all other means of explaining those things. They therefore took it for granted that they were spirits, usually in the form of animals or men. Through the smallest crack or crevice the nightmare slips to the sleeping one, and torments and troubles him so sadly that he becomes ill or that it causes his death. It is felt as an oppressing weight upon the breast or throat; the mare "treads" or "rides"

42

the sleeping one from his legs up to his body and thrusts his tongue into the victim's throat to hinder him from crying out. The Northern people have clung to this very day to their belief in the "mare" as a supernatural female being, and many legends about it have arisen. A "mare" can slip out only by the same way that it came in; if one stops up the opening, it is caught. The same thing happens if one names its name.

In the Ynglinga Saga it is told of King *Vanlandi,* who had betrayed his Finnish bride, *Drifa,* that he in punishment for that had been killed by a "mare" with which the magic arts of the Finns had tormented him. He became suddenly sleepy and lay down to rest, but when he had slept a little he cried that a "mare" was treading him. The king's men hastened to his assistance, but when they turned to his head, the "mare" trod upon his legs so that they were nearly broken, and if they went to the legs, she was directly occupied at the head; and so the king was actually tortured to death.

3. DREAMS.—The part that *dreams* play in the popular consciousness is well known. In our fathers' poetry every great event is presaged by dreams, through which fate in some way is revealed to men. Baldur had evil dreams before his fateful death, and in the Icelandic sagas and our Danish folk songs we meet dreams at every turn. Souls can even in one's lifetime forsake the body and wander far and wide, as it transpires in dreams. Such a soul is called in the old language *hugr,* 'thought' or 'soul'; it took on the most varied forms of beasts, appearing most often as a bear, a wolf, or an eagle. A man dreamed that he was going out from one of his buildings and there he saw some wolves come running from the south in upon the field; there were eighteen in all and a she-fox was running on ahead. When he was awakened he knew immediately that they were *manna hugir,* 'men's souls,' which boded an approaching battle. The holy Bishop John's "soul" was often occupied with what belonged to the divine service, both before the Bishop fell asleep and before he awoke.

Draumr-Draugr.—From the same root as the word "dream" (Old Norse *draumr*) is also the old word *draugr,* which means now soul as specter, now has the same meaning as *hugr.* (The

common basal meaning seems to be "to press, squeeze." Therefore the older language used also the verb "to dream" in a peculiar construction; for example, this man has often "dreamed
me"—originally = has often tortured me as "mare" while I slept;
later = has often presented himself to me in dreams.)

4. FORM SHIFTING.—A kindred relation is presented by our
fathers' widespread belief in *form shifting,* i.e. the soul's ability
to leave the body and assume another form, *hamr.* In the
Ynglinga Saga it is told about Odin, that he "changed his form;
the body lay there as if heavy with sleep or dead, but he himself
was in the form of a bird or beast, fish or worm, and went in a
twinkling on his own or another's errand to distant countries."
Freyja has a falcon cloak or form, the Valkyrs flew in swans'
form, the giants oftenest in the form of eagles.

Hamram and Berserk.—Men who had a peculiar aptitude for
changing form were called *hamramir,* "strong in form." We must
certainly regard the fury of the Berserk as in the same category.
Warriors who in the heat of battle were attacked by wild and
brutal frenzy were called *Berserkir* or *Ulfhethinn, i.e.* men who
wear furs or bear or wolf skin; but the original belief was really
that they went about in the form of bears or wolves.

5. GHOSTS.—But it is especially the souls of the dead that
"haunt." Older Norse literature abounds in evidences of a belief
in ghosts. They most often return to the dwelling they had while
in the flesh, or they move about preferably in the vicinity of
their burialplace. Frequently the spirits occasion only evil when
they reappear, and the surviving must withstand dangerous con-
flicts with them, until they are properly "put to rest," *i.e.* lodged
in a mound of heaped-up stones.

The renowned Icelandic chieftain, *Olaf Paa,* at *Hjartharholt,* had
many servants. One day the man who took care of the farrow horned
cattle came and asked to be released from that work, as he would
rather do something else. Olaf thought that he should perform the
work that was given to him, but the man preferred to seek another
place for himself. Olaf then went with him at evening to the cow stable, which was a long way from the farmyard, to investigate the cause
of the trouble. The fellow received orders to bind the creatures fast
after Olaf drove them in. He now went in at the door, but instantly

rushed back into his master's arms before the latter could look about him. Olaf asks then why he acts so awkwardly. He answers, "Hrap is standing in the stable door and is groping for me; but I have had enough of wrestling with him." Hrap was an evil-tempered Iceland farmer, who, after his own wish, had been buried standing under the door of one of his houses so as to be better able to oversee his property, and who afterward had worried the whole neighborhood by appearing and haunting the locality. Now Olaf goes in at the door and thrusts after Hrap with his spear; the point breaks off meanwhile and the apparition vanishes into the earth. The next morning Olaf went to the place where Hrap had been "put to rest" and had him exhumed. He was even then not decayed, and Olaf found his spear-point also with the body. This was now burned and the ashes were cast into the sea. Then, for the first time, the people in the neighborhood had peace.

Spirits in Popular Tradition.—At times it was interest in the surviving which brought the spirit back to earth. He returns to expiate a fault, or from longing to see again his loved ones. Later we shall tell about *Helgi, Hunding's Bane,* who in the tomb receives a visit from his beloved Sigrun. (Folk songs about Aage and Else, and Lenore.) Here also belongs the widespread popular tradition of *The Wild Hunt,* outlawed spirits who in dismal forms on headless steeds and with their own heads under their arms at night-time drive through the air. From Denmark we know *Abel's* hunt at Schley and *Valdemar's* at Gurre; Norwegians tell about *Aasgaardsrei.*

6. The Dead are Conjured.—From belief in souls the idea quite naturally developed that the souls of the dead could also be called back to earth against their will, according to the wishes of men. One can conjure them up when one knows the right charms to use. In the Eddic Song about Baldur's Dreams, Odin rides down to the underworld to the grave of a prophetess, chants potent *valgaldir* or charms over the dead, who then steps forth and speaks "the death-word." *Svipdag,* the hero in another Eddic Poem, goes to his mother *Groa's* grave and calls her forth to his aid. *Hervar* conjures up her father *Angantyr* from the tomb on *Samsö* and compels him to deliver up the sword *Tyrfing.* Belief in conjuration is very ancient and common to all people using our group of languages. It seems as if our older

poetry especially has contained magic songs of different kinds, among others some for this use.

7. FUNERALS AND FUNERAL- OR GRAVE-FEASTS.—Even from the earliest times, our forefathers took particular care for the burial of the dead. They gave them the necessaries for their continued life, sometimes simply necessary objects for use, sometimes splendid implements and ornaments. We can trace a distinct development from the grave-finds of the Stone and Bronze Ages to the moor-finds of the Iron Age and the buried ships of Viking times. But also from historic times we have good evidence of our fathers' burial customs. We must understand the *erfiöl*, 'funeral feast,' as a kind of offering to the departed at which people originally thought of the spirit as present and honored it by regaling themselves with meat and drink—a custom which is faithfully preserved at the burial feasts of the common people. At the funeral feasts the heir for the first time occupied the high seat of the deceased and completely assumed his dignity; then was brought forward also the "Bragi cup" over which they made their vows. (Ceremonies of the *Jomsvikingar* and Svein *Tiuguskegg.*)[1]

So long as the body was not buried, the soul remained near by. Therefore they removed it from the house as soon as possible, preferably the same day that death occurred. First they rendered *nabjargir*.[2] They approached the dead person from behind, stretched the body out and closed the eyes, after which the face was covered. Then the body was placed in a mound, lying or sitting, and richly supplied with implements and weapons. *Gunnar* from Hlitharendi laughed and sang in the tomb. When the son *Hogni* seizes his renowned father's spear to undertake blood-vengeance, the mother of the dead asks who ventures to touch the weapon. Hogni answers: I intend to take it to my father so that he can have it with him at Valhalla and exhibit it at the weapon-show. People usually chose open and nicely situated burial places on mountains or hills, or in forests.

---

[1]Jomsburg Vikings and Svein Twibeard, early king of Denmark. See the Hcimskringla.
[2]Last service to dead.

But criminals and trolls who especially did evil as ghosts were "put to rest" or burned. The mound and monument upon it are called in the old language *Kumbl. Bautarsteinar*[1] (memorial stones without inscriptions) and rune stones have been discussed above.

8. WORSHIP OF THE DEAD.—It is difficult to say definitely whether there was among our forefathers a complete system of ancestor-cult, *i.e.,* worship of the dead in the family; but there are many who maintain that this usage prevailed from a very ancient time all through the heathen age. The forefathers of the race were considered the family's natural protectors in the spirit world, and many passages in the old literature relate about offerings to the dead either in or at grave-mounds or family-mounds, or upon adjacent mountains. Sacrifice was made to a man named *Grim* after his death, because of his popularity, and Snorri plainly understood Frey as an earthly prince who later was worshiped as a god.

9. TRANSMIGRATION OF SOULS.—There is also much that goes to show that our heathen forefathers had a widespread belief in the *transmigration of souls.* The soul of the deceased could take its abode in a newborn child and live another life. Those human beings thus reborn are called in the old sources *endrbornir,* 'born again,' Helgi, Hjorvarth's son, and the Valkyr Svafa were *endrbornir.* Of the renowned Helgi, Hunding's Bane, a prose piece in the Elder Edda relates: "The belief prevailed in ancient times that people became *endrbornir,* but now it is called old wives' talk. Also about Helgi and Sigrun, it was said that they were born again." Saint Olaf was, after the opinion of people, one born again from a traditional-historical king, *Olaf Geirstathaalf,* who received sacrifice. To the belief in being born again was perhaps attached originally the custom of naming a child after one deceased in order that the one concerned might be born again in the little child who bears the dead person's name.

----

10. INDEPENDENT "SOULS."—In the course of time new religious ideas were developed from soul-belief; namely, a belief in

----

[1]*Bautar* from *bautathr* means 'fighter' or 'hero.'

independent supernatural soul-beings whose life and activity are not dependent upon the particular human body.

a. *Fylgjur.*—A transition from the belief in souls and the worship of souls in the simplest form, to supernatural soul-beings, forms our fathers' faith in the soul as a guardian spirit. The soul is man's *fylgja*, 'attendant,' from the cradle to the grave, and since it can forsake the body and put on a new form, it is also called *hamingja*. Originally, then, the *fylgja* is quite the same as *hugr*, which in dreams or in waking condition, in its own or another's form, can manifest itself especially as a warning of great events or of near approaching death. To see one's own *fylgja* is a certain sign that death is near. This feature is preserved in the superstition of the present time where the vision of one's self or another as a corpse or as occupied with a corpse is regarded as a death-warning. *Fylgjur* appear in the same manner as *manna hugir*, oftenest in animal form, according to a person's character. Great chieftains and men of note had "strong" fylgjur which walked in front of them, but which could be seen by only a few specially gifted persons.

When Thorstein Uxafot[1] was a boy of seven years, he once came quickly rushing into the room, as children are wont to do, and fell on the floor. Wise old *Gejt* saw it and burst out laughing. So the lad went to him and asked why his falling appeared to him so laughable. "Well," said the old man, "because I saw it as you did not see it. When you entered the room a white bear's cub followed you and ran before you on the floor; but when it set eyes on me it stopped, and when you then came hurrying in you fell over it." It was Thorstein's *fylgja*, and Gejt concluded from that that he was not of ordinary origin.

b. *Fylgjur as Women.*—The next step in the development of the belief in tutelary goddesses is this, that one can lend another his *fylgja*. Powerful persons, or those known for their especial good fortune, bestow their fylgjur upon those whom they wish to help. Fylgjur here resemble good luck, and besides hamingja the old language uses also, in the same sense, other words which ordinarily have the general meaning 'good fortune.'

---

[1]Oxfoot.

The Icelander *Hjalti Skeggi's* son drove with *Bjorn Stallare* to Sweden on an errand for Olaf the Stout. On leaving he said to the king, "And we now greatly need, O King, that you give your hamingja for this journey." Olaf answered among other things, "You shall know for a certainty that I shall bestow all my *hugr* in case it weighs anything in the scale, and give my hamingja to go with you and all of you." Here the king unconsciously indicates how the pretty and implicit belief developed among our forefathers. The king's *hugr, i.e.* his good wishes and thoughts for the journey, follow them; but this is interpreted as if the king's second *ego*, his *hamingja* or *fylgja* set free, as a kind of luck goddess, follows them on their way.

c. *Family Fylgja.*—More plainly does the fylgja appear as an independent soul-being in its capacity as *aettar-fylgja*, 'family fylgja,' which cares for the fortunes of the family and takes up its abode now with one, now with another, of the members. After its owner dies, the fylgja seeks an abode with another person, preferably one of the same family. When Christianity was introduced, the opinion seems to have developed that one could *change his fylgja together with his belief.* The old chieftain Hall let himself be baptized by *Tangbrand* on condition that the archangel Michael should for the future be his fylgja.

The scald, *Halfred,* upon his death-bed on board his ship did not wish to have the company of his fylgja over into the next life. Then the people saw a woman walking along the ship, handsome to look upon and dressed in a coat of mail; she went over the waves with the same readiness as if she were walking on the ground. It was Halfred's "fylgja-woman," or fetch, from whom he now had freed himself. Another man to whom she applied did not wish to have her, either, but finally she was accepted by the poet's son, and in this way remained in the family.

d. *Dream-Women.*—As a being set free, the *fylgja* is also called *Dis, Spadis,* or *Draum-Kona,* who makes her appearance to help men. She then closely resembles the Norns and Valkyrs who are also plainly designated as *Disir,* who upon Odin's command summon heroes home to Valhalla.

11. NORNS AND VALKYRS.—The conception of fate-women and battle-women as personal, divine beings has developed from the soul-belief among all the Gothic Germanic people, but

Norns and Valkyrs represent a distinctly Northern development. The first word is found only among Norsemen, the other with Anglo-Saxons as well; on the other hand *Wurd* (Norse, Urth 'spinning woman'?) as a name for inexorable fate is found among all racially related people. In our fathers' belief there are many Norns, good and evil, who "wind fate-threads" and fix man's life from the cradle to the grave.

Valkyrs are the "Norns of Battle," but among our people they have received their character from Odin faith and the teaching about Valhalla. They serve at table in Valhalla and they "choose the slain," the *Val*, at Odin's command, when as well-equipped shield-maidens they take part in the conflict and determine its course. A series of pretty myths about Odin's divine maids has arisen in Norwegian-Icelandic mythology and poetry. (The "Darrath Song"[1] in Njal's Saga; *Hakonarmal*.)

The Valkyrs appear often with half-human nature, since they contract marriage with earthly heroes, until the battle nature suddenly awakens in them and drives them away from hearth and home into the tumult of conflict. As *swan-maidens* they fly far across the country. At times they lay off the swan form in order to bathe; but if this is stolen by a man, the maid must follow him and give him her love (cf. section on Hero-Sagas).

12. WITCHES.—In the Eddic Song *Havamal*, Odin enumerates in a special section the magic songs he is able to use. In this it says:

HAV. 155
This I know, the tenth,   If I see witches[2]
hurry through the air;
I so arrange   that (they) go deprived
of their own shape,   of their own home.

Our forefathers had then a widespread belief also in evil soul-beings, peculiar souls of the witches of the earth, who after death continue their evil dealings with men. Such evil spirits are designated by various words, as troll, sprite, night-creature, evening-, darkness-, and farm-rider.

---

[1]Weaving Song of the twelve Valkyrs: a 'Battle' Song.
[2]Lit. Farm-riders.

13. NATURE-DEMONS.—Again, the belief in *elves, dwarfs,* and *gnomes* seems to have grown out of soul-worship. Originally these names designated only souls which had taken fixed abodes out in nature and were in possession of certain qualities and accomplishments in advance of men. In the later myths these beings play an important part and belief in them has been preserved a very long time among the common people. With these must also be classed such supernatural beings as *goblins, river-sprites, mermen,* and *mermaids,* which form a transition to the real nature-demons.

Giants.—The common names for nature-demons are giants, frost and mountain giants. While elves and dwarfs especially bear the imprint of the calm, mild, and friendly in nature, giants are symbols of the forces of nature and the elements in their might and fury, the worst enemies of mankind, with which a hard struggle must be carried on in order to insure existence. Ordinarily giants are thought of, therefore, in wild and dismal forms, corresponding to the elements by which they are surrounded; but giant women may after all be very handsome, so that they even awaken love in the breasts of the gods. Njorth was married to the giant Thiazzi's daughter Skathi, and Frey's affection for Gerth, daughter of Gymir, is treated in one of the finest of the Eddic Songs. To what is told about giants in the first section, we will add some individual examples from the giant's world.

14. AEGIR AND RAN.—The foremost sea-giant is *Aegir* or *Hler,* who, according to Snorri, has his dwelling on Hlesey.[1] He is indeed a giant but he is on terms of hospitality with the gods, for whom he arranges great banquets. It was at one of these that Loki took occasion to pour out his venom upon the gods and goddesses. The billows are called Aegir's daughters. His wife is named *Ran,* and she catches shipwrecked men in her net, with which she may cruelly pursue the seafarer. To Ran come all who suffer death upon the sea by accident; according to the testimony of a certain saga it is the sign of a good reception at the home of Ran, when the drowned man obtains leave to turn back to

---

[1] Island of Hler, now Laesö in the Kattegat.

take part in the funeral feast which is held for him. Loki borrowed Ran's net to catch the dwarf *Andvari,* who in the form of a pike was darting around in a waterfall.

Another more violent sea-giant is *Hymir,* at whose home Thor sought the great kettle of which we shall tell in a later paragraph.

II. Chief Gods and Myths of the Gods
(THOR)

1. WORSHIP OF ODIN AND THOR.—Attention has already been called in the general introduction to the fact that Thor was the Norseman's real chief divinity from a very ancient time, and that his name "the Thunderer" designates only a single side of the God of Heaven; but he was later understood to be an independent, personal being. Odin worship is far younger and made its way north from a Germanic people dwelling farther south. In the consciousness of the common people, conceptions of Thor as the supreme god were never superseded; but Odin faith received full and pleasing development in Norse-Icelandic poetry.

Thor as Chief God.—Thor was at one time the chief divinity with all the Gothic-Germanic peoples. Not only does the general occurrence of the symbol of the hammer bear witness to this, but also the fact that he is placed by the side of Jupiter, since Jupiter's day is rendered by Thor's day. An old Low-German baptismal formula begins as follows:

> "Do you renounce the devil—
> and all offerings to the devil—
> and all the works of the devil?"
> "I renounce all the devil's works and words,
> *Thunar* and *Woden* and *Saxnot* and all the
> Trolls which are worshiped here."

Thor, Odin, and "Saxnot" (the one armed with the sword) are precisely the three chief gods who are most often named in Norse sources, provided we can identify Saxnot with Frey. It is at the same time not solely the significance of the name and the hammer-symbol, or the testimony of rune stones, which tell us about the extent of the worship of Thor. The same testimony recurs in names of persons and places, in which we find Thor in overwhelming abundance, compared with Odin and Frey. Where heathen temples are mentioned, statues of the chief gods in them are sometimes named, and in that case Thor's name ordinarily comes first, as in the baptismal formula above. Most often a temple of Thor only is mentioned, or a representation of Thor alone. The Yule-offering, the chief offering of our heathen forefathers, was consecrated to Thor, and Thor's day appears as the most important week-day in all legal questions; the court was opened on a Thursday, and Thursday is the most common court day even now. Norwegian-Icelandic poetry itself gives here and there unmistakable evidence of Thor's prominent position.

2. MITHGARTH'S KEEPER.—The Volva's Prophecy in its description of Ragnarok in the verse cited on page 39 calls Thor, as Mithgarth's Keeper,[1] "Veurr." *Veurr*, related to the Danish word *vie*, 'to consecrate,' and to *Ve*, 'sanctuary,' signifies protector and consecrator, and Mithgarth is certainly the land of human beings. Other poets call him *Friend of Human Kind* or *Defender of the Race*, and he occupies a similar position even among the gods, who constantly seek protection through his strength even if Odin or Frey is present. Therefore he is called *Asa-bragr*, the most prominent of Aesir. Thor is consecrator and protector of all human life; he thereby becomes the protecting divinity not merely of the individual man, but also of the home and the state. He is the great god of civilization, with the strongest and mightiest powers at his command, the lightning— the hammer, *i.e.* the thunderbolt—which crushes and splinters whatever offers resistance (desolate nature in giant forms) but which also brings with it fruit-producing rain.

3. CHARACTERISTICS OF THOR.—People most often picture Thor to themselves as a strong middle-aged man, rarely a young man, but in both cases he has a glowing red beard. He is tremendously strong; his flaming glance is enough to terrify any

---

[1] Or Defender.

one, and he is dreadful in his wrath, but under ordinary circumstances he is gracious and mild. When he, in his wagon drawn by he-goats, drives over the sky, this is in flames and the mountains tremble or burst in the thunder's crash. The modern Danish *Torden,* 'thunder,' means 'Thor-rumbling,' like the older Danish form; the Swedes say *aska,* the word being a contraction of *as-eka,* 'driving of As.'

To Thor's name there are attached a number of myths or divine traditions, and of these we shall now recount the most important.

4. THE GOD'S TREASURES.—Of the origin of the god's treasures, Snorri relates the following: Loki had once from malice cut off the hair of Thor's wife *Sif.* When Thor became aware of it, he wanted to crush every bone in Loki's body; but the latter promised to get golden hair from the dark elves for Sif in compensation. He applied therefore to the dwarfs, who are called the sons of *Ivaldi,* and they upon his demand made hair for Sif, the spear *Gungnir* which Odin received, and the ship *Skithblathnir* which could sail over both sea and land but could also be folded together and carried in a pouch, in case one preferred. This good ship Frey received. After that Loki wagered with a dwarf *Brok,* staking his head that the latter's brother *Sindri* could not complete three equally good treasures. Brok plied the bellows and Sindri forged, and although Loki in the form of a gadfly three times stung the one plying the bellows and forced him to stop a moment, Sindri notwithstanding finished the three great pieces of work: the boar *Gullinbirsti,* the ring *Draupnir,* and the hammer *Mjolnir.* Loki with his stings accomplished only this, that the hammer handle remained a little too short. The wager was to be settled in Asgarth. Thor took the hammer, Odin the ring, and Frey the boar, after which these three gods were to pronounce judgment. The hammer decided the matter, and Loki was now to lose his head. He ordered Brok to take it, but the neck must not be touched, since the wager applied only to the head itself. In exasperation, the dwarf then sewed Loki's wily mouth together.

5. THE HAMMER IS RECOVERED.—One of the oldest Eddic Songs relates how Thor lost his hammer and recovered it. Angry

awoke Ving-Thor and missed his hammer; his beard and hair
shook; the son of Jorth groped around, but the hammer was lost
and could not be found. Loki, to whom the god of thunder
describes his loss, borrows Frey's feather garment and flies over
to the king of the giants, *Thrym*. The latter admits having concealed the hammer deep in the earth, and he will not give it
back unless Freyja is brought to him as his bride. Loki flew back
and the demand of the king of the giants was communicated to
the goddess of love, but

THRKV. 12
Wroth grew Freyja,   and she fumed,
all the Aesir's hall   trembled therefrom,
there bursts that great   Brisinga chain[1];
Thou knowst me to be   most mad for men,
if I drive with thee   to Jotunheim.

The Aesir and *Asynjur*, 'goddesses,' assembled for delibera-
tion at the court to consider how the hammer could be regained.
Heimdall solves the problem: "Let us bind bridal linen about
Thor and give him the great Brisinga ornament to put on; keys
shall rattle at his girdle, women's garments fall about his knees,
head and breast be decked in woman's fashion." Thor must submit to the hard necessity, for the giants will take possession of
Asgarth if he does not regain the hammer. Loki, Laufey's son,
also dresses in women's clothes, so as to follow Thor as his maid
upon the strange bridal journey.

21
Soon were the goats   driven homeward,
hurried to the traces,   they must run well;
mountains burst,   earth burned with fire,
Odin's son drove   into Jotunheim.

In Jotunheim there is prepared a splendid bridal feast, but
Thor is ill adapted to the bride's part. At first his ability to eat
and drink awakens amazement, nay, almost terror, in Thrym;
and when the bridegroom lifts the veil to kiss his bride, he darts
back terror-stricken the length of the hall, for Freyja's eyes are

[1]Necklace.

sharp and shine like fire. The artful bridesmaid meantime comforts him with assurance that the goddess's appetite and piercing glances were due only to her yearning for the bridegroom, since she had neither eaten nor slept in eight days.

THRKV. 30

Then quoth Thrym   the giants' chief:
Bear in the hammer   to bless the bride!
Mjolnir place   on the maiden's knees,
bless and join us   by the hand of Varr.

Now comes the hour of reparation and vengeance for Asgarth's mighty god:

31

Laughed Hlorrithi's   heart within his breast,
when he, hard-hearted,   the hammer perceived;
Thrym he slew first,   the giants' chief,
and the giant's race   all he crushed.

The wretched sister of the giant had begged for a bridal gift; she received a hammer-blow instead of golden rings. After this the thunder-god returned to Asgarth with his recovered weapon.

The same theme is treated in a jesting manner in the ancient Danish ballad about *Tor of Havsgaard.* Tor of Havsgaard rides over green meadows and loses his golden hammer. Lokke Lojemand (jester) puts on the feather cloak and seeks out the *Tossegreve,* 'foolish count,' who has hidden the hammer and will not give it back unless he gets "Jomfru Fredensborg (Miss Peacecastle) with all the goods she has." After this, Tor and Lokke, as in the Eddic Song, must put on women's clothes and proceed to the Tossegreve's land. Tor's appetite in the ancient ballad is quite astonishing—he ate a whole ox and thirty hams; no wonder that he was thirsty after that! But when the hammer was brought in, it was evident that he could use it, and the Tossegreve with all his tribe were crushed. The ballad ends thus:

Lokke said this, crafty man,
he did consider it well:
Now we will fare to our own land,
as the bride has become a widow.

6. HYMIR'S KETTLE.—Thor one time, relates the Lay of

Hymir, had to go to the giant Hymir for a great kettle which was to be used at a feast for the gods at the home of the sea-god Aegir. He sets out together with Tyr, and they reach the giant's dwelling. The latter does not come home until towards night, and is much offended both at his guests and at Thor's appetite. The following morning Thor goes out with the giant to fish. The god demands bait of the ferocious giant, who asks him to look out for it himself. Thor then wrenches the head from one of the giant's black oxen, after which they begin to row. Hymir is frightened at Thor's violent strokes and objects to keeping on for fear of coming upon the Mithgarth serpent. This, however, is exactly Thor's purpose, and while the giant is attending to his affairs, Thor makes the "Earth-Encircler" swallow the hook and draws his head up to the surface of the sea. At the same moment when he wishes to crush his skull the terror-stricken giant cuts the line and the monster sinks back safe upon the bottom of the sea. This adventure has again and again inspired our forefathers. One of the very oldest Scalds gives a graphic picture of how the "Earth-Encircler," like a wildly floundering eel, gazes defiantly from the depths below up at the "Cleaver of the Giant's Skull," who is only waiting to give him the fatal blow (cf. Fig. 19).

In Snorri, Thor in his godlike strength breaks through the planks of the boat until he gets a footing on the bottom of the sea. As the giant has hindered him in his purpose, Thor hurls his hammer after the serpent and chastises the giant with a frightful box on the ear, after which he himself wades ashore. The poem on the other hand has them both turn back together, just as they went out. Thor, however, may not now obtain the kettle until he can further prove his strength by crushing the giant's beaker. That does not break until the god hurls it against the owner's own skull, after which he snatches the kettle and carries it from the court, pursued by the giant's hosts, which he crushes with his hammer.

7. HRUNGNIR.—The myth of Thor and *Hrungnir* has been very widespread and popular, and the Scalds often alluded to it; but in connected form it is preserved only in Snorri. Once when Thor was in the East in order to crush the trolls, Odin seated himself upon Sleipnir and rode to Jotunheim. Here he met the

giant Hrungnir, who boasted that his steed *Gullfaxi* was far better than Odin's. Odin rode back to Asgarth, but the giant followed him even into the dwelling of the gods. Now drink was borne before him, but when his boasting become too arrogant, the gods called upon Thor, who quickly appeared and was on the point of crushing the giant. The latter intimated that it was only a slight honor to slay a defenseless foe; he must rather meet him in a duel at the frontier, where Hrungnir would then appear with shield and grindstone. Such a challenge Thor did not allow to be offered twice, and the giant went away satisfied. As help

Fig. 19.—Thor's Fishing.

for him the other giants built now a champion of clay, nine rasts high, and three rasts broad between the shoulders. He was called *Mokkrkalfi,* and he had a mare's heart in his breast; Hrungnir's heart was a three-cornered stone. At the appointed time Thor made his appearance, attended by *Thialfi.* The giant stood with the shield before him and the grindstone in his hand. At the same time Thialfi went forward and called to him that Thor was coming from below, after which Hrungnir stepped upon his shield and grasped the grindstone with both hands. Thor meanwhile went forward through the air amidst lightning and crash of thunder. The grindstone and hammer were hurled at the same time and met midway; Mjolnir holds its course and crushes the giant, but half of the stone strikes Thor in the forehead so that he falls to the ground in such a way that the giant's foot lies across his neck. Thialfi strove with the clay giant, who trembled with fear and fell with little glory. Meanwhile no one could lift the giant's leg away, until Thor's three-year-old son *Magni* came up; he then received Gullfaxi as a reward for his strength, although Odin himself had meant to have that good steed.

When Thor came back to Thruthvang, the healing woman, *Groa,* was brought, who recited magic songs over him until the stone began to sway in his forehead. Snorri adds that it did not, however, get completely loose, for Thor told Groa that her husband, *Orvandil,* was coming home presently. Thor had borne him on his back in a basket over the poisonous streams on the return journey from Jotunheim. One of his toes, however, was frozen off, and Thor had cast it up to heaven and made it into a star. But Groa became so joyful at this information that she forgot her witchcraft.

8. GEIRROTH.—Loki had once been caught by the giant *Geirroth,* to whose court he had from curiosity betaken himself in Frigg's falcon cloak. In order to get free he had to promise to bring Thor to Geirroth without his hammer or his strength-belt. In this the artful Loki was easily successful, but on the way Thor visited the giantess Grith, Vithar's mother. She instructed him about Geirroth and lent him at parting her strength-belt, her iron gloves, and her staff. Thor came first to a brook in which

one of the giant's daughters had occasioned an inundation. He slew her and escaped to land by drawing himself up into a mountain ash. In Geirroth's hall there was only one chair, and it went up quickly as far as the ceiling when Thor seated himself upon it. He then pressed against it with Grith's staff and pushed with all his might, after which there was heard a great roar, for the giant's daughters had been under the chair and lay there now with broken backs. On the floor there was kindled a great fire, beside which people took their seats. Geirroth then seized a glowing iron wedge and cast it at Thor, who caught it with the borrowed gloves, after which the giant hid himself in terror behind a mighty iron pillar. Thor now hurled the wedge with such force that it pierced through the pillar and Geirroth also, and went out through the wall on the opposite side. The main source of this myth is the obscure Scaldic lay *Thorsdrapa,* which is retold by Snorri.

9. THOR'S JOURNEY TO UTGARTH.—In Snorri is also found the late adventure of Thor's journey to *Utgarth,* which probably is the best known. This tale attained great celebrity after Oehlenschlaeger made use of it as the basis for his poem, "Thor's Journey to Jotunheim,"[1] the introduction to "Gods of the North."[2] Snorri's long account is a free and fanciful transformation of a whole series of Thor-myths now for the most part lost.

  a. Thor gets Thialfi and Roskva from the peasant (Egil).
  b. The meeting with Skrymir (the gloves, lunch bag, Thor's hammer-thrust).
  c. Utgarthaloki (the eating test and the race. Thor drinks from the sea, lifts the Mithgarth serpent, and wrestles with Elli, *i.e.* Old Age).
  d. The optical illusion is removed and Thor wishes to take vengeance, but without success.

10. ALVIS.—An entirely characteristic but not very transparent myth lies also at the basis of the Eddic Song of *Alvis.* Alvis is a dwarf who, without its being evident wherefore and from whom, has received the promise of Thor's daughter. He now

---

[1]Tors Rejse til Jotunheim.
[2]Nordens Guder.

comes to take her, but is addressed with scornful words by Thor. The dwarf does not know him and asks him to mind his own business; only when he is informed who Thor is does he become humble and tell his errand. Thor, however, will not give him his daughter unless he can answer all questions in accordance with his name, "The All-wise." Now the interrogation begins, Thor asking the dwarf how different things, *e.g.* the sun, moon, earth, are named by gods, elves, dwarfs, giants, and other mythical beings. The dwarf is remarkably well informed but does not give heed to the time; he is overtaken by the day and turned to stone before the beams of the rising sun.

11. Thor-Faith Long Prevalent.—When the vigorous priest Tangbrand preached Christianity in Iceland, he once fell into conversation with a heathen woman, who said to him, "Have you heard that Thor challenged Christ to a holm-going (duel fought on a holmr, 'islet'), but Christ dared not contend with Thor?" This tale is significant as to our fathers' first view of the new doctrine, and it really proved that the old ideas were preserved among the people long after the introduction of Christianity. It was especially difficult to eradicate the faith in the protecting and consecrating virtue of Thor and his hammer. The sign of the hammer and the sign of the cross were confused, indeed were even placed side by side as sacred symbols in

Fig. 20.—Figure of Thor (?).

Christian churches (Fig. 20). In Norway, strange to say, the common people transferred not a few of Thor's qualities to Saint Olaf. From the Norwegian peasant's King Olaf, with flaming red beard and with ax in hand, the sorcerer's bitter foe, to the red-bearded thunder-god with the hammer, who crushes the giants' and mountain giants' skulls, is a leap not nearly so great as one at the first glance might think. But with the Christian priests, Thor and Odin naturally stood as the worst among all the evil beings of the heathen days; for them Christ and Thor are as incompatible as good and evil. It is this contrast which Oehlenschlaeger brings out in the famous conclusion of the third act of "Hakon Jarl":

OLAF.   Heaven will strike thee with its flames!

HAKON.   Thor shall splinter the cross with his hammer!

ODIN

1. WORSHIP OF ODIN.—Together with Tyr and Thor as well as the goddess Frija ('the beloved,' Mother Earth), *Odin* is a common Germanic divinity, and this can be proved also by philology. Tyr's original significance as the ancient god of heaven is, in the North, completely obscured; the sources relate nothing particular about him beyond that which is stated in the foregoing. Odin's name signifies "the one blowing," and the relation here is quite the same as in the case of Thor; a single side of the god of heaven is thought of as a person and an independent divinity. Odin's worship is, as we have already remarked, somewhat young in the Northern lands; but since it permeates all Norse-Icelandic poetry, we must now look a little more closely at Odin's divinity and the myths which are attached to him.

2. ODIN'S APPEARANCE AND SURROUNDINGS.—Odin is thought of as an old, tall, one-eyed man with a long beard, broad hat, and an ample blue or parti-colored cloak. On his arm he wears the ring Draupnir, on his shoulders sit the ravens Huginn and Muninn, 'Thought' and 'Memory,' and at his feet lie the two wolves, Geri and Freki, 'Greedy' and 'Eager.' Ordinarily he is armed with the spear Gungnir, and rides upon Sleipnir (he has many other horses, among them the war-horse Blothoghofi),

and he often travels as a wanderer around the world with staff in hand.

Odin's Names.—If we sum up all of Odin's names in poetry, we have more than two hundred; the most of them signify one or another characteristic of the god: All-father, the Blustering, the Changeable, the Stormer, the Wanderer, the Traveler, the Gray-bearded, the Bushy-browed, the Helmet-bearer, the Great Hat, *Valfathir,* 'Father of the Slain,' *Herfathir,* 'Father of Armies,' King of Victory, King of Spears, the Terrifier, God of Burdens, *Fimbultyr* ('Mighty God'), God of the Hanged, and Lord of Spirits (*i.e.* ghosts). From these examples alone it will appear that Norwegian-Icelandic poetry represents Odin as the world's chief divinity. But the clearest picture of him is that of *God of Wisdom and the Art of Poetry, and in theories about Valhalla, as God of War.*

3. ODIN, GOD OF WISDOM.—First of all Odin acquired his wisdom by personal investigation: he traveled through all countries and had wide experience. But in other ways also he gained information, for the ravens fly every morning out over all the world and bring tidings back with them, and in heaven there is—besides his castle *Valaskjalf* or *Valhalla*—also a place *Hlithskjalf,* a castle or simply a high seat, from which Odin can look out over the whole world. We have already heard what sacrifice Odin was obliged to make in order to increase his knowledge at the time when he had to pledge one of his eyes to obtain a drink from Mimir's well of wisdom.

4. VAFTHRUTHNIR.—In the Eddic Songs about *Vafthruthnir,* Odin is described as the most prominent God of Wisdom. Odin is speaking with Frigg; he has a desire to visit the wise giant Vafthruthnir, to test his sagacity. Frigg advises him to remain at home, but Odin answers:

VAFTHR. 3
I have journeyed much,   attempted much,
I have tested oft the powers;
this I wish to know   how Vafthruthnir's
household may be.

He departs, accompanied by Frigg's best wishes, and comes to

the giant's hall, where, under the name of Wanderer, he chal-
lenges the latter to a contest of wisdom. First of all Odin, standing, answers the giant's question about the steeds of day and
night, the boundary river *Ifing* between the countries of gods
and giants, and the plain *Vigrith*. Then quoth Vafthruthnir:

VAFTHR. 19

Wise now thou art, oh guest,   pass to the giant's bench
and let us talk on the seat together!
Wager our heads   shall we two in the hall,
oh guest, upon our wisdom.

After that the song rehearses a number of the main points of the
belief in the gods in questions on Odin's part; but the giant
never hesitates about an answer, until the god asks him, "What
did Odin say in Baldur's ear before he was borne upon the
pyre?" Then Vafthruthnir understands with whom he has
engaged in contest.

55

No man knows this,   what thou in early days
didst say in thy son's ear:
With fated lips   I uttered ancient lore—
and of the downfall of the gods.

5. GRIMNIR.—There was once a king by name *Hrauthung*, who had
two sons, *Agnar* and *Geirroth*, of whom the first was ten, the second
eight winters old. These two rowed out with a boat to fish, but the
wind drove them off over the sea, and in the darkness of the night they
were stranded upon a foreign shore. Here a man and woman met
them and cared for them during the winter. The peasant (the man)
took charge of Geirroth and gave him good counsel, while his wife preferred Agnar. In the spring they went away in a boat, but the peasant
whispered something first to his foster-son. When the boys came to
their father's anchoring ground, Geirroth sprang quickly ashore, thrust
the boat out again, and called out to his brother, "To the Trolls with
thee!" after which the boat again drove out upon the sea, while
Geirroth went up to the royal castle and later became an illustrious
prince. The foster-parents were, however, not poor people, but Odin
and Frigg. Now, as they were sitting one time in Hlithskjalf,
Odin taunted his wife on account of Agnar and his fortune, to which
she answered that Geirroth was, to be sure, a king, but he was so

niggardly about food that he tormented his guests in case too many came. Odin declared this to be untrue, as indeed it was, wagered upon his opinion, and set out in order to inquire into the matter for himself. But Frigg sent her maid to King Geirroth and warned him against a man versed in magic who was to come to his court and who could be known by this, that dogs did not dare to bite him. Soon afterward a man came in a blue cloak, and called himself *Grimnir,* "The Masked"; the dogs shrank back before him, wagging their tails, upon which the king gave orders to seize him and place him between two pyres so as to force him to say who he was. There he sat eight nights. Then the king's ten-year-old son Agnar had pity on him and brought him a filled horn to drink. Grimnir drained it, while his cloak caught fire, after which he began to speak.—Thus it is told in the prose introduction to the Sayings of Grimnir. The poem itself contains a number of disconnected names and myths, of which we shall quote a single one.

6. SACA.—Odin is enumerating the dwellings of the gods. Here he says among other things:

GRIMN. 7
Sokkvabekk the fourth is called,   and there do cool waves
go rushing over;
there Odin and Saga   drink every day,
cheerful from golden cups.

This Saga has been understood as a kind of Muse of History, since the name has been associated with the well-known words, "a saga." Philologists, however, have pointed out that this conception cannot be correct. *Sokkvabekk* should really be rendered 'Sinking Bench,' and *Saga* is doubtless a name for Frigg, according to which the myth is an allusion to the sunset, a poetic expression for the sun-god's meeting with Frigg, when the sun every day sinks below the horizon westward into the sea.

Frija, Frea in the Norse language, grew into Frigg, one of the few Germanic female divinities that can be pointed out. Originally she was married to the god of heaven TiwaR, but when Odin supplanted him he came into possession of his maid and his wife. Furthermore, in Norse mythology, she is readily confused with *Freyja,* for which reason it is difficult to determine which myth concerns the one or the other. It is most likely that Freyja, 'the Ruling One,' was only an epithet of the queen of heaven and was later made into a new divine being. Of the other names of the queen of the gods can be mentioned *Jorth, Fjorgyn, Hlothyn.* Friday means originally Frigg's day, just as the constellation Orion was first called Frigg's, but later Freyja's, Spinning-wheel.

7. GEFJON.—Probably *Gefjon* also is originally from one of Frigg's names. In the Eddic Song *Lokasenna* (the Loki Quarrel), Odin says that Gefjon knows the destiny of the world as well as he himself. Far better known, however, is Snorri's account of *Gefjon and Gylfi.* King Gylfi in Sweden gave her as much land as she could plow about in one day with four oxen. She brought her four giant sons and transformed them into plow oxen, but this team plowed so deep that the land was loosened, whereupon the oxen drew it out westward into the sea. It is now called Zealand, and the headlands correspond to the inlets of the sea which remained behind in Sweden, where the land had been.

8. THE MEAD OF THE SCALDS.—The myth about Odin acquiring the *Mead of the Scalds* has, briefly, the following content: *Scaldship* (poetry) is represented as an inspiring drink; he who partakes of it is a Scald. It was kept at the home of the giants, where Gunnloth guarded it. Odin makes his way through all hindrances, gains Gunnloth's affection, and gets permission to enjoy the drink. He then carries it up to the upper world and gives it to men.

In the oldest and purest form the myth appears in the Eddic poem, Havamal: "The man must be gifted in speech who wishes to know much and to attain anything in the world. This I (*i.e.* Odin) proved at the home of the giants; it was not by keeping silent that I made progress in Suttung's hall. I allowed the auger's mouth to break me a path between the gray stones. The giants were going both over and under, so it was by no means without danger."

HAV. 105

Gunnloth gave me   on the golden seat
a drink of the precious mead;
ill return   I later let her have
(for her faithful heart)
for her troubled mind.

106
Her well-gained beauty   have I much enjoyed,
little is lacking to the wise;
since Othrerir   is now come up
to verge of men's abode.

107
Doubt is in me   if I had come again
out of the giant's court,
if of Gunnloth I had had no joy,   that goodly maid
who laid her arm about me.

108
The day thereafter   the frost-giants went
(to ask of Har's condition)
into the hall of Har;
for Bolverk they inquired   if he to the gods had come
or had Suttung him destroyed?

109
A ring-oath, Odin,   I think, has sworn:
who shall trust his good faith?
to Suttung deceived   he forbade the drink
and he made Gunnloth weep.

Snorri's account embraces the following essential points:

a. After the truce between the Aesir and the Vanir, each of them spat into a vessel, and from this fluid they made, as a token of peace, the man *Kvasir,* who was very wise. Kvasir was slain by two giants, *Fjalar* and *Galar,* who caught his blood in the kettle *Othrerir* and two vessels. The blood they mixed with honey, and from this arose the mead of the Scalds.

b. The two giants now invited another giant, *Gilling,* and his wife to come to them. Gilling was drowned while on a sailing party, and when his wife grieved about it they slew her. The son, *Suttung,* wanted to take vengeance for his parents, but agreed to accept the mead of the Scalds as compensation, and set his daughter, Gunnloth, to guard it within the mountain.

c. When Odin set out to gain the mead he came first to a field where nine slaves were mowing grass; these were *Baugi's,* Suttung's brother's men. Odin offered to whet their scythes, and the whetstone was so excellent that they all wanted to buy it. The god then cast it up into the air, but all were so eager to grasp it that they killed each other in the attempt. After that Odin, who called himself *Bolverk,* proposed to Baugi that he carry on the work of the slaves with this as reward, that he receive a draught of Suttung's mead. To this Baugi agreed.

d. When the time for work was at an end Suttung, however, refused to fulfill his brother's promise, but Bolverk thus took advantage of the fraud: he gave Baugi an auger and made him bore into the mountain where the drink was hidden. It was not long before Baugi declared that the hole was through; but when Bolverk blew, he got chips in his face, and the crafty Baugi had to bore again until the chips flew inward. Now Bolverk proceeded into the mountain in the form of a serpent, won Gunnloth's love, and received the promise of a drink of the mead for each of the three nights he was there. He drained then in three draughts both the kettle and the vessels and flew in an eagle's form toward Asgarth.

e. Suttung discovered this and pursued him, likewise in eagle's form. When they drew near to Asgarth the gods set out their vessel so that Odin might spit out the mead into it, but the giant was close upon him and some of the mead then went the wrong way; this, which the gods did not collect, became the portion of the rhymsters and the poor Scalds.

REMARK.—Othrerir was perhaps at first the name for the mead of the Scalds itself.

9. RUNES.—The old word "rún" signifies mystery, secrecy. It was not long before the runes themselves—at first certain of them, later all of them—were interpreted as magic signs, and faith in the mighty runes has long been maintained in popular belief and in poetry (cf. old Danish ballads). No wonder, then, that the discovery of runes was ascribed to Odin himself. This is distinctly told in several Eddic songs, but the real meaning is difficult to discover.

Odin is then also the god of all sorcery, wherefore he is called *galdrs fathur,* 'Father of Magic Song,' and by the later Christian church in the North was regarded as the worst of the evil beings whom the heathen worshiped.

In the "Heimskringla" an account is given of how Odin, as an old one-eyed man, with his broad hat, came to King Olaf Tryggvason when the latter was at a feast at court. He talked long and shrewdly with the king and was surprisingly well acquainted with old traditions, with which he entertained the king even after the latter had gone to bed. At his departure he gave the steward fat horse-shoulders to roast for the king. In due time, however, the old man's deception was discovered.

10. ODIN AS GOD OF BATTLE.—"As god of war and battle Odin enters into the life of men. War is his work; he arouses it. He incites kings and earls against each other. The warriors are driven by a higher spirit. This he fosters by teaching his favorites new means of conquering, and he himself mingles in the battle to help them or bring them to himself (Harald Hildetann). All those who die in arms belong to him. He gathers only nobles about him, so that there can still be heroes when the last great battle is at hand."

Of Valhalla, the Valkyrs and Einherjar an account has already been given.

FREY AND NJORTH

1. WORSHIP OF FREY.—The third chief divinity among the people of the North, about whose worship we have definite information, is *Frey,* who, however, cannot with certainty be pointed out as a general-Germanic divinity and whose nature and origin therefore are difficult to determine. The name signifies *The Ruling One.* The corresponding feminine form is *Freyja,* 'The Mistress,' whose name heretofore was preserved in Danish in the word *Husfrø,* which later through German influence became *Husfru* and after that was changed to *Hustru,* 'wife.' The general mythological details about Frey have been given above, where too his significance as the supposed ancestor of the Swedish race of kings is indicated. The *Ynglings* in Sweden descend, according to an old Scaldic lay, from Yngvi-Frey. Through this name we can perhaps trace a connection with Germany, since the Latin historian Tacitus in his *Germania* names three chief Germanic races, of which one was the *Ingvaeones.* In any case Frey is originally a variation of the god of light and heaven. He himself is called The Shining One, God of the World, and Chief of the Gods. He lives in Alfheim; his boar is called *Gullinbursti,* 'golden bristles,' his attendant

Skirnir, 'Maker of Brightness,' and he is in possession of treasures which only the most prominent god can own.

According to the Volva's Prophecy he contends in *Ragnarok*
with *Surt.* There he is called *Beli's Blond Destroyer. Beli* is
brother of the giantess *Gerth* and one of the finest of the Eddic
poems, *Skirnismal,* 'Skirnir's Journey,'[1] deals with Frey's love for
Gerth.

2. SKIRNIR'S JOURNEY.—Skirnir is Frey's attendant but also his
friend from youth up. Wherefore he is quite accustomed to
being the god's confidant. One time something was troubling
Frey, for he seated himself apart without wishing to speak with
any one. Skathi then bade Skirnir ascertain what had awakened
the strong god's wrath, and Frey answered:

SKM. 6
In Gymir's court   I saw walking
a maiden dear to me;
her arms shone   and from them too
the air and all the sea.

7
A maid dearer to me   than maid to any man
youthful in early days;
of Aesir and of elves   this no one wishes
that we should be together.

In the prose introduction to the poem it is related that Frey
had seated himself in Hlithskjalf and had looked out over all the
world. He had also cast eyes upon the fair Gerth, daughter of
the giant Gymir.

Skirnir offers now to ride to Jotunheim as a suitor for his
friend, provided the latter will lend him the steed which will
bear him most safely through the dark, flaming magic fires, and
the sword which swings itself against giants and trolls. This is
done, and after a dangerous and intricate ride the swift Skirnir
stands in Gymir's hall in conversation with Gerth. Without cir-
cumlocution he tells his errand; first he promises her eleven
golden apples, next, the ring Draupnir, provided that she will

---

[1]Indicated by the title *For Skirnis* often used.

give Frey her love. He is however refused on both scores, for "gold is cheap in Gymir's court; I have the disposition of my father's wealth." Then Skirnir resorts to threats: he will strike her father down and slay her with the rune-written sword; with the magic wand he will subdue her and send her as booty to the cruel troll-people of the underworld.

SKM. 33
Wroth with thee is Odin,   wroth the most excellent of gods,
thee shall Frey hate;
Most evil maid! (thou) who hast attained
the gods' ferocious wrath.

34
Hear ye giants,   hear, frost-giants,
ye, Suttung's sons,
(ye gods too)
how I forbid,   how I deny
to the maid   the joy of men
to the maid   the pleasure of men.

The maid who can reject the bright, beaming god's affection shall be punished by becoming Hrimgrimnir's bride down in the death-realm. Thither shall she totter every day, broken in will and without volition, partake of the most loathsome food and live her life under the most gruesome conditions. Not until now does the stubborn maid submit, terror-stricken.

38
Hail (now rather), youth!   and take the crystal cup
full of ancient mead;
yet I have ne'er believed   that e'er I should
love well a Vanir's son.

But Skirnir wishes to have full information and Gerth answers then that in nine nights, in the grove *Barri*, she will celebrate her bridal with Frey. Then Skirnir rides back to the latter and tells him the result of his journey. The poem ends with Frey's declaration of his inexpressible longing for the bride.

3. FREY-NJORTH.—It is well understood that there is a definite connection between Yngvi-Frey, Freyja, and Njorth, but

the original relation has not been successfully determined. Both Njorth and Frey in Norse mythology are gods of fruitfulness and have about the same characteristics. The most of these are found also in Freyja. Tacitus mentions in connection with a North German tribe a female divinity Nerthus, and with this name the Norse word *Njorth* exactly agrees as a masculine form. Upon an island in the ocean was her sacred grove, with a consecrated wagon which only the priest might touch. In this wagon drawn by cows, the goddess in solemn procession and amid the exultation of the people was led about on festal days. Then peace and joy prevailed. Before the goddess was taken back to the temple, the wagon, the garments, and the divinity herself were washed in the sacred lake.

REMARK. The tale about *Hertha* and her worship at *Lejre* (in Zealand) is only a late tradition which is founded on a perversion of Tacitus' account, and does not belong among the heathen beliefs.

HEIMDALL AND BALDUR

1. HEIMDALL is a purely Norse divinity and must according to his name and peculiarities be, like Frey, a manifestation of the god of heaven and light, perhaps more definitely the god of the morning red, the day's gleam which shows itself at the horizon immediately before the rising of the sun. The name means "he who lights the world." His steed is called Gulltopp. An account has been given above of his dwelling and employment. The Volva's Prophecy begins with the following words:

VSP. 1
Hear me all   ye holy kindred,
greater and smaller,   Heimdall's sons!

That men are here called Heimdall's sons is not necessarily an outcome of an ancient conception of Heimdall as supreme god. This expression comes rather from an Eddic song which is somewhat older than the Volva's Prophecy, in which the god, under the name of *Rig*, is represented as the ancestor of the different classes of society.

2. RIG is a Celtic word which means prince or king. Long ago the wise god, strong and active though advanced in years,

wandered along green paths until he came to the hut in which great grandfather and grandmother, *Ae* and *Edda,* dwelt. He took a situation with them, gave them good advice, and partook of their heavy coarse bread and soup. He remained there three nights and sought rest between them. But nine months afterwards Edda bore a child, which was baptized with water and received the name *Thraell.* He had a furrowed skin, long hands, an ugly face, thick fingers, long heels, and a stooping back; but he became great and strong and capable for work. Later he married Thir, "a thrall," and from the two descended all the Thralls.

Rig wandered farther along the road and came to a hall which grandfather and grandmother, *Afe* and *Amma,* owned:

RIGSTH. 15
The couple sat there,   were· busy with their work;
the man was hewing there   wood for a weaver's beam;
his beard was trimmed,   a forelock on his brow,
shirt was close fitting,   a chest was in the floor.

16
The woman sat there,   turning her distaff,
stretched out her arms,   made ready the cloth;
a coif was on her head,   kerchief on her breast,
a scarf was at her neck,   clasps upon her shoulders.

Filled dishes and cooked veal were set upon the table. Rig ate and remained there three nights, and nine months later Amma bore a son, who was baptized and called *Karl.*[1] He tamed oxen, forged tools, built houses, and tilled the ground. His wife was called *Snor,* and their progeny was the race of free peasants.

Rig continued his wandering until he reached the hall of father and mother, with the door towards the south, a ring in the door-post, and the floor covered.

RIGSTH. 27–8
The householder sat   twisting his bow-string,
bending the elm-bow,   fitting the arrows,
But the housewife   was observing her arms,
stroking her dress,   drawing tight her sleeves,

---
[1]Free man.

her cap set high,   medallion on her breast,
had long trained-dress   and bluish sark.

The mother laid a white-figured cloth upon the table and set on
fine wheat bread.

31

She set dishes   silver-plated on the table,
well browned bacon,   roasted fowl;
wine was in the tankard,   the cups were of fine metal,
they drank and talked,   the day was nearly done.

But afterwards mother bore a son who was swaddled in silk,
baptized, and named *Jarl.* "Light were his curls, bright his
cheeks, sharp as a serpent's his shining eyes." Jarl from childhood had practice in arms. Rig came to him, taught him runes,
called him son, and gave him great riches. *Erna* became his
wife, and they had many valiant sons, of whom the youngest was
Kon ungi ('Kon the Young,' hence *Konungr,* the word for
"king"). He was a glorious hero and vied with or surpassed Jarl
both in arms and in shrewdness. Finally he set out for adventure
in order to gain celebrity and a fair bride in Denmark. The
poem consists here of incomplete fragments only, yet we hear
that

RIGSTH. 38

The shaft he shook,   he swung his shield,
his steed he urged,   he drew his sword;
strife he did awake,   the field he reddened,
warriors he felled,   gained land in war.

The Lay of Rig contains undoubtedly a glorification of kingly
power and is supposed to have been composed in Norway in
praise of an absolute king (Harald Harfagri?[1])

3. BALDUR.—The myth of Baldur, the most disputed of all the
myths, is also distinctly Northern. Baldur is commonly understood to have arisen, like Frey and Heimdall, from an embodi-
ment of an original epithet of the old god of heaven. Bugge, on
the contrary, maintains that the theories about Baldur are

---

[1]Harald Fairhair, king of Norway, 860–933.

formed from a combination of Irish legends about Christ and misunderstood Greek and Roman tales. This view, however, encounters great difficulties, and strong opposition to it has arisen. (See Introduction.)

4. TWO BALDUR MYTHS.—Besides allusions in several Eddic songs, we find the Baldur myth in various forms in Snorri and Saxo. Both in Denmark and elsewhere in the North, place-names are found and local traditions which are connected with Baldur. The plant-name "Baldur's brow" also is an evidence of the faith in this god.

The substance of the myth is the same in Snorri's and Saxo's representations: Baldur is a son of Odin and Frigg; he is slain by Hoth but is avenged by his brother. Hoth signifies "combat" and agrees closely with the form *Hotherus* in Saxo, who, however, calls the avenging brother *Bous,* the Vali of Icelandic sources. In Saxo the contest turns upon the princess Nanna, King Gevar's daughter, who is loved by the Shielding[1] Hother, while with the Icelanders she is the god Baldur's wife, and Hoth is his blind brother. In Saxo there are preserved indistinct traits of the Valkyrs (the three Forest Maids) and of the murderous sword which is kept by the giant Miming. We must also remark that as Baldur is everywhere a son of Odin, the information about him must at all events be later than the rise of Odin faith and is therefore of comparatively late development.

5. BALDUR'S DREAMS.—In addition to all we have alluded to concerning Baldur in the preceding section we will now recount a few Icelandic myths about this god.

Since evil dreams had given warning of danger to Baldur's life, Odin rode upon Sleipnir down to Helheim to the burial place of a wise sibyl. With powerful incantations he conjured up the dead and asked her for news from the underworld; in return he agreed to tell her about earth and heaven. He wants to know why such festal preparations are being made in the hall of Hel: the floor is spread with straw, the benches strewn with rings, and the wagons filled with clear drinks and covered with shields.

---

[1]Shieldings, Icel. *skjoldungar,* lit. 'sons of Skjold,' came to mean 'princes,' 'kings.' Heathen kings of Denmark were meant.

The sibyl confirms his gloomy forebodings: it is Baldur's coming that they await.—This is the chief content of the Eddic Song of Vegtam[1]; but the conclusion of the poem is incomplete and unintelligible.

6. BALDUR'S FUNERAL.—The Aesir took Baldur's body and carried it to the sea. *Hringhorn* was the name of Baldur's ship, the largest among all ships. The gods wished to push it out and make Baldur's funeral-pyre upon it, but the ship could not be moved. They then sent a messenger to Jotunheim for a sorceress who was named *Hyrrokin*. She came riding upon a wolf and had a viper for a bridle. Four Berserks were to guard the wolves, but they could not hold them until they had thrown them down. Hyrrokin went to the bow of the ship and pushed it out with the first thrust, so that fire went out from the rollers and the whole country trembled. At that Thor became wroth, grasped the hammer, and wanted to crush her head, but all the gods united in saving her by their intercession. Now Baldur's body was borne out upon the ship. When his wife Nanna saw this, her heart broke from grief and she was laid upon the pyre with her husband. Thor next stepped forward and consecrated the pyre with the hammer. A dwarf ran before his feet and Thor in his rage kicked him into the fire, where he was burned. Many gods and giants were present at the funeral. Odin laid the ring Draupnir on Baldur's breast, and the god's horse was led out with all his trappings.

7. HERMOTH'S HEL-RIDE.—After Baldur's death, Odin's son, Hermoth the Swift, took it upon himself at Frigg's request to ride down to Hel to beg release for Baldur. He saddled Sleipnir and rode nine nights and days through dark and deep dales; he could not see a hand before him, until he came to the river *Gjoll* and out upon Gjallar Bridge, which was covered with bright gold. *Mothguth* was the name of the maid who watched the bridge. She asks him for his name and race and says that the day before there rode five companies of dead men over the bridge, "but not less does the bridge resound under you alone; you have not the color of dead men; why do you ride hither upon the

[1]*Vegtamskvitha.*

Hel-road?" Hermoth asks if she has seen Baldur; she answers in the affirmative and shows him the way: "down towards the north goes the Hel-road." Now Hermoth rides farther, until he comes to Hel's grated gate. He dismounts from his horse, girds him fast, mounts again, gives him the spurs, and the horse leaps over without touching the gate at all. Then Hermoth rides on to the hall and goes in. He sees his brother Baldur sitting in the high seat, but remains there over night before he discharges his commission. At his departure Baldur sends gifts to Odin.—How the test of weeping failed has already been told.

8. THE DEATH-REALM.—The narrative about Hermoth's Hel-ride deviates widely from Snorri's descriptions in various places of the realm of death and the goddess of death, but contains certainly an older and more original conception. Hel means "the concealing one." She is a queen and dwells in splendid halls which are decorated like a royal castle on earth, for the floors are strewn and the benches covered with carpets and expensive materials. Dead men (but neither those dead of disease nor cowards) *ride* to Hel in warlike hosts and all equipped, and their king takes his place on the high seat which is prepared for him. Conceptions of Hel as a place of punishment are not at all definitely indicated in the oldest poetry, yet on the contrary a *Nifl-Hel* is named "to which men die from Hel." The oldest belief seems to have comprehended three worlds (although the Volva's Prophecy tells of nine): the land of the Gods, the World of Men, and the Realm of the Dead (heaven, earth, and the underworld, possibly with a hint at a place of punishment, Nifl-hel). But when the Odin-cult and with that the belief in Valhalla first made its way into the popular consciousness, men thought that the brave went to Valfather, the cowardly, and those dead of disease to Hel. Then Hel became Loki's daughter and her realm a counterpart of Valhalla.

Hel, according to Snorri's representation, gained sway over nine worlds in Niflheim. Her kingdom is called *Helheim,* which is reached by the Hel-road, over the Gjallar Bridge, past the Hel-gate or death boundary. The Hel-hound, Garm, runs out of the Gnipa-cave. The death-goddess herself, horrible to behold, is upon her throne in the hall *Eljuthnir,* her maid is *Ganglot,* her threshold is called "falling deceit" and her couch is the "bed of sickness."—The word Hel is even now preserved in the Danish words *ihjel*, 'dead'; *Helved*, 'hell'; *Helsot*, 'fatal disease'; and *Helhest*, 'hell-steed.' Likewise the widespread superstition that the howling of dogs presages death is probably a half-extinct reminder of the Hel-hound.

LOKI

1. LOKI.—We have now remaining one of the most enigmatic figures within the circle of Norse gods, the one who bears the name *Asa-Loki*, although it is often recorded that he originally belonged to the race of giants. Many explanations have been given of the meaning of the name, and just as many of the origin and meaning of the god himself. It is most probable that Loki signifies "the one closing, bringing to an end," and in order to understand his nature we will begin with his own words in the old lay, The Loki Quarrel:

LOK. 9
Dost remember, Odin, when we in early days
did mingle blood together?
Taste ale you never would, you vowed,
unless 'twere borne to both.

Loki is accordingly Odin's foster-brother and in the most intimate and cordial relation to the chief divinity possible between two men. He has also many of Odin's noble qualities, but his temper is such that he is not capable of exercising them in the right way. He has sense and understanding like Odin, but they express themselves in bitter malice and fraudulent acts. He is as strong in merits as in faults, but the latter gain more and more control. Odin's foster-brother, Asa-Loki, must therefore become finally the worst enemy of gods and men, who also at Ragnarok takes a commanding position among the evil powers in the destruction. Hence he is endowed in the later mythological poetry with one evil trait after another. With *Angrbotha* he begets the frightful trio, and since he also occasions Baldur's death, it is with a certain right that he has been called the "devil of the North."—On the basis of his relation with the storming heaven-god, Loki might properly be regarded also as the god of fire, and for this a strong argument may be found in the narratives about him. Fire is the benefactor of the human race, but also its merciless enemy. Thus Loki becomes the opposite of Heimdall, and with him he fights the last battle at the crisis of the gods, just as he previously at *Singasten* had fought with him for Freyja's necklace, Brisingamen.

2. SEIZURE OF ITHUN.—One time the three Aesir, Odin, Hœnir, and Loki, traveled from home over fields and desolate lands where they could find no food. First, down in a valley, they found a herd of oxen, of which they killed one and sought to cook it over a fire; but the flesh would not become tender, however much they cooked it. This was caused by an eagle which was sitting in a tree above them, and which said it must have its full share of the ox should the cooking succeed. The gods promised this, but when the meat was cooked the eagle took both thigh and shoulder for his part. In exasperation at this, Loki thrust at him with a rod, but the rod remained fast in his body and Loki was unable to loose his hold on the other end. The eagle flew rapidly and high; Loki's limbs were almost torn from him before he yielded. It was the giant *Thiazzi* in eagle's form who had borne him away. For his freedom he was now obliged to promise to entice away Ithun with the Aesir's old-age remedy (the Apples), so that the giant could seize her. At the time agreed upon Loki coaxed Ithun out into the wood with her apples, in order that she might compare them with some others that he claimed to have found. The giant then came up in eagle's form and flew away with Ithun.

But when Ithun was away the Aesir soon turned gray. Ithun was last seen together with Loki, and the latter in order to save his life had to confess everything and promise to restore the goddess to Asgarth. In Freyja's falcon-cloak he flew rapidly to Jotunheim, found Ithun at home alone, transformed her into a nut, and flew away with her in his claws. Shortly afterwards Thiazzi came back and missed Ithun. In eagle's form he pursued the robber, who, however, escaped over Asgarth's walls, behind which the gods had kindled a great fire. With scorched wings, Thiazzi sank to the earth when he could not stop his mad flight, and was slain by Thor.

3. SKATHI IN ASGARTH.—Thiazzi's daughter Skathi now put on full equipment and proceeded to Asgarth to take vengeance for her father. Meanwhile, to reconcile her, the gods offered to allow her to choose for herself a husband from their number; but she was to choose according to the feet alone, for the body and head she was not allowed to see. She chose then a man with very handsome feet, in the belief that it was Baldur, but it proved to be Njorth. Their experience has already been related. Skathi was even now not satisfied and demanded that the gods should make her laugh. No one was able to do this but Loki, at whose wanton jests she could not keep serious. As additional penalty Odin (or Thor) took her father's eyes and cast them upward to heaven, where they were transformed into stars.

4. LOKI SCOFFS AT THE GODS.—Loki's worst offense was this, that he caused Baldur's death; but as we have seen, he had time and again defied the gods before. He offered them the greatest disdain at the feast which the sea-giant Aegir instituted for the Aesir and for which Thor had brought the great kettle from Hymir. All the gods and goddesses were present with the exception of Thor, and Loki also took part in the feast. Aegir's two servants received much praise for their swiftness, but Loki was provoked at this and struck one of them dead, after which he was driven out. Some time afterwards, however, he returned to the hall and now began to scoff at the gods and goddesses, the first with mockery and sarcasm, the latter with venomous words in which he charged them with a lack of chastity. Some sought to quiet him, others retorted, but all in vain. He stood there in the midst of the hall as the Aesir's evil conscience. To be sure, he exaggerated strongly; but there was a grain of truth in all he said, and therefore they all sat there well-nigh distracted. At last Sif, Thor's wife, became the object of his scoffing. Then they called on Thor, and the strong god stood there in the hall brandishing his strength-hammer; three times Loki ventured to defy Vingthor, but when the latter the fourth time threatened him with death, he fled:

LOK. 64

I spoke before Aesir, spoke before Aesir's sons,

that which my mind did prompt me;
but before thee alone,   shall I go out
since I know   that thou dost strike.

Such is the main content of the Edda-song of Loki's Quarrel
(Lokasenna).

THIRD SECTION

Forms of Worship and Religious Life

1. KINGS AND CHIEFTAINS WERE PRIESTS.—The general administration of the Norse kingdom and the performance of the acts of religious worship formerly devolved upon one person. The king was the "Guardian and Protector of the Altar," and it was his duty to see that everything in religious matters proceeded properly and in order. He had charge of the sacrifices of the kingdom, and if any unlucky year came over the land, there were cases where he himself even was sacrificed for the attainment of better conditions. As the king's representative the Jarl kept up the sacrifices on the king's behalf in the different provinces. The smallest division of the country, the *herath* (Lat. *centuria*), was governed by the *Gothi* (from *goth,* meaning "god"), whose name clearly signifies that his functions were of a religious nature. The institution of the Gothi is known especially from Iceland, from which country as usual we get the best information; but similar conditions probably prevailed throughout the North. In any case we meet the word *Gode* upon a few Danish rune-stones—on one with the addition, "The honored servant of the holy places." An actual priestly *office* like that among the Egyptians or the Gauls, our forefathers hardly knew. A *"thulr"* is mentioned on a Danish rune-stone on the hills of *Sal* (the village Sallov near Roskilde). This word means "Speaker, Wise-man," but it is not possible to determine what is really meant here by this designation, and perhaps it has no religious meaning at all.

2. TEMPLES.—Originally the Germanic peoples certainly had

no *buildings* for their religious services, but worshiped the gods in the open air, especially in sacred groves such as Tacitus describes in his *Germania*. But it was not long before the whole race of people learned to build temples, probably from a foreign model. The temple of heathen antiquity in the North was called *Hof* or *Horg*. The last word means in general "a holy place," but perhaps signifies the especial temple of a goddess. The Hofs were large square, occasionally round, houses, built in the same style and of the same kind of material as the common dwelling houses, very nearly like the guild-halls of the chieftains. They faced west and east, and had a circular recess at one end in which the images of the gods were set up. In most cases the temple was of wood, comparing in size with village churches in Denmark, and surrounded by a fence. The first Christians immediately transformed the Hof into a church, after the images of idolatry were put away and the place was consecrated. It is needless to say that they employed all the splendor and art which the times allowed. Gold and silver, woven carpets, and carved columns were hardly lacking in any Hof. Often the Hof was built in or by a sacred grove.

3. INTERIOR OF THE HOF.—Just inside the door of the Hof stood the posts of the high seat, in which were fixed great nails, but the meaning of these is not known. At the opposite end (the *Korrunding* or apse) stood the images of the gods, and in front of them or under them the splendidly ornamented *Stall*, which one of the Icelandic sagas compares with the Christian altar. Upon its iron-covered upper side burned the sacred fire which must never be extinguished, and there also lay the open silver or gold ring upon which all oaths must be sworn. The ring was moistened in the blood of the victim, and on all festive occasions the Gothi had to wear it upon his arm. Upon the Stall stood also a large copper bowl with a sprinkler (*hlautbolli* and *hlauttein*). In the bowl the blood of the victim—animal or man—was caught and sprinkled over those who were present. The Stall also, perhaps the whole interior of the temple, was reddened with it. The statues of the gods were most often clumsy images carved from wood (*skurthgoth*, meaning 'carved gods'), and were set up on the Stall or upon a pedestal, and dressed in

accordance with the festal costume of the period. That there was always a hammer in the hand of Thor's image there can be no doubt.

4. SACRIFICE.—The heathen word for sacrifice is *blot,* and *blota* means 'to sacrifice.' The gods were worshiped with bleeding victims—in the older time, human beings, generally prisoners or bondsmen; later, beasts, the flesh of which was eaten by those taking part in the sacrifices. As a matter of course an individual man or a single family could institute private sacrifice, and of this many accounts exist. In general the *blot,* 'sacrifice,' was regarded as a public act and a religious festival, conducted by the highest chieftain of the place.

Hofs in Norway.—In the Heimskringla there are given—especially in the sagas of the two Olafs—not a few details about the heathen temples and the sacrifice.

Hakon Jarl had been forced to accept Christianity and to take priests with him to Norway. He put them ashore at the first opportunity, and when he himself reached home he went ashore and made a great sacrifice. "Then there came flying two ravens and they screamed loudly; the Jarl thought that he might know that Odin had accepted the sacrifice, and now the Jarl had a favorable opportunity to fight."

King Olaf Truggvason went with his army to Northmaer[1] and christianized the people. Afterwards he sailed to Hlathir,[1] had the Hof broken down, and took all the goods and all the costly ornaments from the Hof and from the gods. He took from the door a large gold ring which Hakon Jarl had had made, and after that caused the temple to be set on fire. The same king also proceeded harshly against the peasants of Trondelag. He went into their Hof at More, accompanied by a few retainers and peasants. "But when the king came where the gods were, Thor was sitting there and was the most honored of all the gods, decorated with gold and silver. The king lifted his gold-inlaid ax, which he had in his hand, and struck at Thor so that the latter fell down from the Stall. Then the king's men sprang forward and thrust down the other gods."

Shortly before this, at an encounter at More, where the peasants had invited him to take part in the sacrifice, King Olaf pronounced the following characteristic words:

---

[1]Now Nordmore and Lade.

"We have then agreed that we should meet here at More and make a great sacrifice. But if I join with you in sacrificing I shall have instituted as great a sacrifice as was ever known—and solely with human beings. And for this sacrifice I shall not select serfs or wretched men, but on the contrary shall make my choice so as to provide for the gods the chief men, and for this I choose Orm Lygra from Methalhus,[1] Styrkar from Gimsa,[1] Kar from Gryting, etc." It is needless to say that the chieftains named who had no men for armed resistance hastened to make peace and reconciliation with the king.

5. CHIEF SACRIFICES.—In the course of the year the Northmen celebrated three principal sacrifices, the midwinter, summer, and harvest sacrifices. The first sacrifice was our fathers' greatest festival, and was observed in January or February. They sacrificed then for good luck and good crops in the coming year, and upon the *sonar-goltr*, or 'sacrificial boar,'[2] they laid their vows concerning the great deeds they wished to accomplish in the course of the year. "After the ceremonies with the victim's blood were performed, the flesh was cooked; the broth was drunk, and the flesh together with the vital parts was distributed to be eaten. In the middle of the floor in the temple there was kindled a fire, over which the kettle hung. The beakers had to be carried around the fire—no doubt the consecrated fire upon the Stall—and with the viands were blessed in commemoration of different gods—certainly of Thor, Odin, and Frey, although Snorri gives a different account." Every peasant who takes part in the sacrifice brings his contribution to the feast; but a chieftain who, at his own expense, holds one of these sacrifices gains great prestige thereby.

6. NATIONAL SACRIFICE.—At a certain period of the year the midwinter sacrifice was observed with especial solemnity in the whole kingdom or large parts of it. For this, also, temples and places for sacrifice were found in different parts of the kingdom (in Denmark, at Ringsted, Odense, and Viborg). We get the best information on this point from Upsala, where a great sacrifice to Frey was held every ninth year. All the men from *Sviaveldi, i.e.*

---

[1]Now Melhus and Gjemse.
[2]Large, choice boar; *sonar* itself means "swine."

the whole Swedish commonwealth, restored thither, and they held an assembly, fair, and market at the same time. Adam of Bremen describes the Upsala sacrifice, which was observed even in his time: "There is held every ninth year at Upsala a solemn sacrificial feast for all the provinces of Sweden. High and low, one and all, send their gifts to Upsala. No one, not even one who may have accepted Christianity, is excused. Offerings are of the following nature: from all living beings there are sent nine males, with whose blood it is the custom to appease the gods. The bodies are hung up in the grove surrounding the temple; there hang dogs, horses, and men all together. A Christian man told me that he had seen seventy-two such dead bodies hanging round about in the trees. Moreover, the ceremonies which are connected with such a sacrifice are manifold and hardly honorable, wherefore it is better to be silent about them."

7. PROPHECY AND OMENS.—Just as the North knew little of any real priestly office, so was there little trace of religious mysteries in the worship in which the whole people openly took part. On the other hand, it was very common at sacrifices to take omens for coming events. This is true of all Northern lands. The expression used was *ganga til frittar*, 'to go to investigate.' The omens were taken in a very simple manner, either from accidental circumstances during the sacrifice or, most often, by drawing lots with small wooden sticks, upon which the necessary signs were made. Besides the clear and simple forms used in public worship, many superstitious ideas were deeply rooted in the consciousness of the people, and we have frequently called attention to these.

Here we should also remember that our information deals only with the last centuries of paganism. It is probable that the chief characteristics of the forms of worship which we have sketched above have a much earlier origin, for a people always adheres with great fidelity to the religious usages inherited from its forefathers. That many more things than we have been able to relate should have taken place at the sacrifices and in the daily worship is perfectly natural. The sagas give an abundance of information about the religious customs on certain occasions, *e.g.* when the *Thing* (assembly) was to be consecrated, at the *holmganga* and other *duels,* and at the institution of foster-brotherhood. Every important act of the individual as well as of the community was, in heathen times, accompanied by religious ceremonies which, generally speaking, were of very ancient origin. Besides this, witches, wizards, and sorceresses played a very prominent part in the daily life. In Norway prophetesses (sibyls) or wandering fortune-tellers enjoyed for a time great reputation.

FOURTH SECTION

Hero Sagas

1. THE HERO SAGA.—The hero saga stands midway between myth and history, since it rests on the heathen conception of life, but also makes use of human experience, frequently even of real persons and events as the basis of a poetic presentation. The hero saga ought, therefore, to be regarded as neither pure mythology nor as pure history. It is free poetical composition which must be judged from a poetical standpoint, but from which we learn to a great extent our forefathers' whole view of life and their ideals. In Northern literature we find an unusually rich and extensive saga-poetry of popular origin. The sagas were not, as with our kindred farther south and with the Roman people, worked over into great art-poems, and the Northern poetry therefore often missed the clearness and coherence which the regulating hand of the poet can effect; but it has on the other hand far greater freshness and fullness. Svend Grundtvig justly expresses his surprise "that with our forefathers in the pagan age, a thousand years ago and more, at a period in many ways both crude and barbarous, there existed the intellectual life and mental power which could produce and develop poetic compositions so admirable and so comprehensive. In richness, power, and depth these do not yield to the ancient Greek, which may indeed surpass the Norse in art as well as in beauty and charm, but quite certainly are inferior in seriousness and moral purity." Since, moreover, this ancient poetry through its original elements has spread more widely than any other among all the Gothic-Germanic people, and since it has become

a rich source of regeneration for the new poetry of the North in the nineteenth century, we cannot close our review of the faith of pagan times without first retelling some of the most widely known hero sagas.

THE VOLSUNGS

2. SIGURTH'S FOREFATHERS.—*Siggi* was Odin's foster son and a noted king. He was slain by one whom he most trusted, and that was his queen's brother. Later his son *Rerir* took vengeance for his death.

Rerir's son *Volsung* had ten sons, among them *Sigmund*, and a daughter *Signy*, who was married to King *Siggeir*. In Volsung's hall stands the broad family-tree, whose branches overshadow the whole house. At Signy's bridal feast a strange old man steps forward and thrusts a mighty sword into the tree; the one who is able to draw it out is to have it. Siggeir tries it without avail, and only Sigmund has the needed strength. Since the former does not wish to give up the sword to his brother-in-law, he departs in ill humor, having first invited Volsung and his sons to a feast at his house. They make their appearance and, although they are warned by Signy, they refuse to flee. Volsung is slain, while his sons are chained to a prisoner's block out in the woods, where nine of them are eaten up by Siggeir's mother in a wolf's skin. Sigmund, on the other hand, is freed with Signy's help and remains many years hidden in the forest. Signy comes to him there in the form of a strange woman and becomes the mother of a son *Sinfjotli*, who, together with his father, burns King Siggeir in his house. Signy voluntarily seeks death in the flames when she has taken vengeance for her family. Sigmund, son of Volsung, after that returns to his native land, where he becomes a famous king. He marries *Borghild*, who with poison kills her stepson Sinfjotli, whose body the father bears away in his arms. He casts off Borghild and soon after marries *Hjordis*, daughter of King *Eylimi*, but is slain after the expiration of a short time by his enemy *Lyngvi*, Hunding's son.

Hjordis, after her husband's death, bears her famous son Sigurd and is taken under the protection of the Viking *Alf*, son of King *Hjalprek*, who marries her. *Sigurd is brought up at the home of King Hjalprek and his sons, but the skillful smith Regin becomes his foster-father.*

3. HREITHMAR'S SONS.—There was a man of the race of dwarfs who was called *Hreithmar.* He had three sons, *Fafnir, Otr,* and *Regin.* The second son, who in the form of an otter caught fish, was slain by Loki once, when the latter was on a journey with Hœnir and Odin. Hreithmar demanded in reparation the otter skin covered with gold. This Loki prepares at the house of the dwarf *Andvari,* who pronounces a curse on both the gold treasure and its owner. Since Hreithmar will not share the gold with his sons he is slain by Fafnir, who after that drives Regin away and in the form of a monstrous dragon lies down to brood over the treasure on the Gnita heath. Regin has meanwhile entered the service of King Hjalprek as a smith, and there he tells Sigurth the history of his family. He forges together the pieces of the sword of Sigmund, Volsung's son, for Sigurth and incites the latter to slay Fafnir. Sigurth promises this, but yet wishes to avenge first his father's death.

4. SIGURTH, FAFNIR'S BANE.—When Sigurth has taken vengeance on the sons of Hunding, he betakes himself, accompanied by Regin, to the Gnita heath. Regin conceals himself in the heather, while Sigurth succeeds in slaying the dragon. He had dug deep channels in the earth into which the monster's blood should run, for fear that otherwise he might be stifled by the poisonous fluid.

Regin now hastens to him and bids him roast Fafnir's heart for himself. Sigurth does so, but when he wants to try with his fingers to see if the meat is done he gets a little of the heart's blood on his tongue, and he suddenly understands the voices of the birds. The chirping of the birds informs him that Regin has evil in his heart and advises him to slay him and to take possession of the whole treasure. Sigurth follows the advice, fells Regin, and takes the dragon's "terror helmet" and the treasure, which he loads upon his horse *Grani,* and then he rides farther (Fig. 21). *Now he has earned his name, Sigurth, Fafnir's Bane.*[1]

---

[1] Icel. *Fafnisbani,* 'Slayer of Fafnir.'

Fig. 21.—Sigurd's Fatal Thrust.

On his way he comes to a mountain, surrounded by flaming fire, but Grani bears him unharmed through the flames. Within upon the mountain lies a sleeping form in full armor. When he turns the helmet back he sees that it is a woman. He cuts the coat of mail asunder and the sleeping woman awakes. It is the Valkyr *Sigrdrifa*, whom Odin has put to sleep. Sigurth and she are betrothed and he rides away.

5. THE GJUKUNGS AND THE NIBELUNGS.—Down in the Rhine country was dwelling at that time King *Gjuki*. His wife was named *Grimhild*, and their children were *Gunnar, Hogni*, and *Guttorm*, and a daughter *Guthrun*. To these "Gjukungs" Sigurth came, established foster-brotherhood with the two elder sons, and after Grimhild had given him a potion to cause forgetfulness betrothed himself to Guthrun. Sometime after that Gunnar wished to sue for the Valkyr Brynhild, whose castle was surrounded by flames. Sigurth accompanied him on his journey, and when Gunnar's horse did not dare to go through the flames, Sigurth assumed Gunnar's form and forced Grani through the fire. The Valkyr, according to a decree of fate, was to marry the one who should accomplish the ride through the fire. Sigurth shared her couch, but a drawn sword lay between them. *Brynhild became after that Gunnar's bride, while Sigurth married Guthrun.*

6. SIGURTH SLAIN.—It was not long before there was strife between the two women. Brynhild begrudged Guthrun the glorious hero as husband for whom she herself had conceived affection. When Guthrun one day imprudently boasted of her husband's superiority and was telling how he had deceived Brynhild, the latter burst out in wrath and injured pride and *she then induced Gunnar and his brothers to slay Sigurth.*

The more particular circumstances of the murder are variously told, but common to all the sources is the thrilling description of Guthrun's great grief and Brynhild's wild, revengeful satisfaction, which is, however, only pretense. Indeed, she confides in Gunnar that Sigurth has fully kept his faith with his foster-brothers but that she on account of her slighted affection has been most hostile of all toward the one she loves the most, and she now induces her husband to slay the hero treacherously. After that she kills herself.

The earliest history of the Volsungs is known only from Northern sources, but in general the Norse and the German versions of the Saga of the Volsungs (Eddic Songs and Volsunga Saga, and the German art-poem, the Nibelungenlied of the beginning of the thirteenth century) agree as far as we have described. With the Germans the hero is named *Siegfried* and his wife *Kriemhild*. But from that point the Nibelungenlied continues with the account of how Kriemhild takes vengeance upon her brothers for her husband's death, while the Norse tradition follows other lines.

7. GUTHRUN AND THE BUTHLINGS.—After the slaying of Sigurth, Gunnar and his brothers took possession of Fafnir's treasure, which later was buried in the Rhine. Therefore the gold is called the "Rhine's red flame." King *Atli*, son of *Buthli* and brother of Brynhild, was embittered at his sister's death, but concluded an agreement with the Gjukungs on condition that he receive Guthrun as his wife. After the wedding he invited his brothers-in-law to visit him, and then slew them in order to come into possession of the Rhine treasure. He had the heart cut from Hogni while living and had Gunnar cast into the garden of serpents. But *Guthrun took vengeance for her brothers* in a frightful way. She slew her two sons and had their skulls converted into drinking-cups, from which she made Atli take a drink mixed with his children's blood. She recklessly told him what she had done, and when he had become intoxicated at the feast she slew him in the night, after which she threw herself into the river, now that she had taken vengeance for her family.

8. GUTHRUN-JONAKR. The later form of the saga *has her rescued in King Jonakr's country.* She marries the king and

becomes the mother of *Sorli, Hamdir,* and *Erp.* These three brothers fall in battle against King *Jormunrek* (Ermanaric), who has had their sister *Svanhild* slain.

In the Nibelungenlied nothing is known of this later development of the saga. However, among the chief characters in the last part of the poem there are introduced *Etzel* and *Dietrich of Bern* (Attila and Theodoric of Verona), and the latter appears frequently in Danish folk-songs which sing of the Story of the Volsungs in close connection with German tradition.

Icelandic poetry has certainly *preserved* the oldest form of the Sigurd Saga, but it is of foreign origin, known to have grown up among the Franks in the course of the sixth century. Sigurd's origin is obscure. He is undoubtedly one of poetry's freely formed ideal figures—but in relation to actual historical events. In the year 437 the Burgundian king Gundahari fell, with large numbers of his people, in a battle against an army of Huns which had marched on to Worms. In 453 Attila, king of the Huns, celebrated his wedding with a young woman named Hilda, but died suddenly during the feast. These two occurrences unite in forming the saga. Hilda is the sister of the Burgundian king, who takes vengeance upon Attila for her brother's death.

THE HELGI SAGAS

9. HELGI HJORVARTH'S SON AND SVAFA.—In Norse poetry there appear besides the common Germanic hero Sigurth, Fafnir's Bane, two heroes of the name Helgi who have no parallels among the Germans. Helgi was a son of Hjorvarth in his marriage with Sigrlinn. He was taciturn and did not answer to any name. One time he was sitting upon a hill, when he saw nine Valkyrs come riding toward him. The most beautiful of them was Svafa, who bestowed on him the name Helgi and encouraged him to warlike deeds by giving him good weapons and promising him her love. Helgi now performed great exploits, after which he made love to Svafa at her father's house. She promised to be faithful to him, and they loved each other dearly.

10. HETHIN.—It so happened at one time that Helgi was on an expedition, while Svafa remained at home with her father, although she was a Valkyr. At the same time Helgi's half-brother Hethin was living at home with King Hjorvarth in

Norway. On Christmas Eve, Hethin was driving home alone from the wood and met on the way a witch who was riding on a wolf and had vipers for reins. She offered Hethin her company, but when he declined it she said, "You will have to pay for that at the Bragi cup!" In the evening they had to make vows, and the chosen boar was led forth. Hethin's mind was so bewildered that he made vows to win Svafa, his brother's loved one. When he had recovered his senses, he repented so sorely that he rode off on wild roads to the south until he met his brother.

11. HELGI'S DEATH.—Helgi received his message with great calmness. "Surely no one could escape his destiny." He had a foreboding of his speedy death, for it was certainly his own *fylgja* his brother had met, in the form of the witch. We had at that time been challenged to a duel by *Alf*, son of Hrothmar, and it resulted as he feared. At *Frekasteini* the brilliant hero is mortally wounded, but in his death-hour he has Svafa sent for and begs her, if she will listen to his words, to forget her sorrow and to bestow her affection upon Hethin. Svafa answers that she will never, because her husband has died with shame and infamy, give her hand to another unknown prince. Hethin then quickly decides the matter; he asks her for a kiss, perhaps the only one and the last, for now he is going into battle and will not turn back before he has avenged Hjorvarth's son, the best hero under heaven.

12. HELGI, HUNDING'S BANE, AND SIGRUN.—In his marriage with Borghild, Sigmund, son of Volsung, had a son who was called Helgi. He soon gained for himself a famous hero's name, especially since he had slain King Hunding, after which event he was called *Helgi, Hunding's Bane*.[1]

There was living at that time a king named Hogni; his daughter was the Valkyr *Sigrun*, whom her father wished to be given in marriage to King *Hothbrodd*, son of *Granmar*. But Sigrun disdained this man and chose Helgi, Hunding's Bane, for her bridegroom. Helgi then went out into the battle with the sons of Granmar, who were aided by Sigrun's father and brothers. He conquered and slew them all with the exception of *Dag*, son of Hogni, who had to make a vow of loyalty to him. Sigrun wept

[1]Icel. *Hundingsbani*, 'Slayer of Hunding.'

much when Helgi brought her the news of her kinsmen's death, but still she was married to the hero. They lived in happy union on the Seva fields[2] and had many children.

13. HELGI'S DEATH.—Helgi, however, did not live to be old. Dag offered sacrifice to Odin to gain vengeance for his father, and Odin lent him his spear. He then sought out his brother-in-law and slew him. When he brings his sister the death message, she is kindled with great wrath at his faithless conduct. Punishment for all the false oaths he has sworn to Helgi shall now overtake him: his ship shall not proceed, if the wind be ever so fair; his horse shall not run, even if foes pursue him hard; his sword shall not bite, unless it sings about his own head. "Only then would Helgi's death be avenged upon you, were you a wolf out in the forest, without goods and without joy, and with no food—only carcasses for nourishment."

Dag seeks to comfort her and offers heavy indemnity. Sigrun rejects everything, but becomes calmer when she remembers the fallen hero.

HELG. HU. 36

Thus had Helgi   put in terror
all his foes,   their kindred too,
as from the wolf   impetuous run
goats from the mountain,   full of fear.

37

Thus had Helgi surpassed   the battle-chiefs
as nobly shaped ash   does the thorn,
or the young stag   dashed with dew,
that towers above   all other beasts.

14. HELGI IN THE TOMB.—The conclusion of this second lay of Helgi, Hunding's Bane, tells about the meeting of Sigrun and Helgi in the tomb. Helgi rode to Valhalla after being entombed here below, and Odin invited him to deliberate with him about all things. At evening Sigrun's maid went to Helgi's tomb. There she saw the hero come riding at the head of many men, and it was some time before she could believe her own eyes: "Is it only

---

[2]Icel. *Sefafjollum:* Sefa, 'affection.'

deceit? I think I see Ragnarok or a ride of the dead. With sharp points you spur your steeds. Has leave to return been granted to the hero?" Helgi calms her and she hastens to Sigrun.

HELG. HU. 41

Go out, oh Sigrun,   from Seva-fell,
if the people's prince   you fain would find;
the marks of battle bleed;   the chieftain begged of you
that the wound-drops   you would stem.

Sigrun goes into the mound to Helgi and says:

42

Now I'm so glad   at our meeting
like the ravenous   hawks of Odin,
when they descry the slain,   warm flesh,
or wet with dew,   the break of day perceive.

43

First I will kiss thee,   lifeless king,
ere the bloody   mail thou lay'st aside;
thy hair, oh Helgi, is   frost-bedecked,
the king is all   moistened with death-dew.[1]

And the prince's hands are as cold as ice. She asks him then if she can do anything for him. Helgi answers:

44

Your fault alone, Sigrun,   from Seva-fell
that Helgi is   with sorrow's dew immersed,
thou, decked in gold, dost weep   with bitter tears,
sun-bright, South's child   ere thou dost go to sleep;
each one fell bloody   on the prince's breast
cold, wet, and burning in,   with sorrow filled.

45

Well shall we drink   the costly mead
though we have lost   our joy and lands;
now are the brides   inclosed within the mound,
the wives of men,   beside us now in death.

Then Sigrun prepares a couch in the tomb for Helgi and says:

---

[1]Blood.

46

For thee, oh Helgi, I've prepared a couch
untroubled quite, oh Ylfing's son;
and in thy arms I wish, oh, prince, to sleep,
as with the living prince I might.

To this Helgi answers:

47

Now nothing I say is unhoped for
late or early at Seva-fell,
since in the arms of me the lifeless one, thou'lt sleep,
white in the mound, oh Hogni's maid!

48

'Tis time for me to ride the reddened ways,
to cause the fallow steed to tread the airy track;
ere Salgofnir[1] may wake the victor-throng.[2]

Helgi thereupon rides away with his men. The following
evening Sigrun wanders about the tomb to wait for her dead
husband. The maid is keeping watch and says:

49

Now were come if so he planned,
Sigmund's son from Odin's hall;
of the king's coming, I say, the hopes grow dim,
since upon ash-limbs the eagles sit,
all people hasten to the court of dreams.

50

Be not so thoughtless that thou far'st alone,
wife of a king, to the abode of death;
more mighty grow at night time all
ghost-like foes than in the shining day.

Helgi came not, and in the course of a long time Sigrun died
from grief. The same pretty theme is treated in the Danish folk-
song "Faestemanden i Graven,"[3] or "Aage og Else."

_____

[1] Cock in Valhalla (Gering).
[2] The Einherjar.
[3] The Bridegroom in the Grave.

VOLUND THE SMITH

15. VOLUND AND HIS BROTHERS.—The sagas of *Volund* (*Volundr, Valand, Velent, Wielant*, etc.) are found among all the Germanic people and have in all probability wandered from them to the Romans. In the saga of Theodoric of Verona a section is found which recounts all of Volund's life. An ancient English poem gives a single episode of his history.[1] The Old Norse poem *Volundarkvitha* likewise treats merely a single section, upon which Oehlenschlaeger has composed his "Vaulundurs Saga."

A Finnish king had three sons, *Slagfith, Egil*, and *Volund*. They went out upon skis and hunted game. One time they came to *Ulvdaler*,[2] and built themselves houses there by a lake which was called *Ulvjar*.[3] Early one morning they found on the shore three women who were spinning flax. They were Valkyrs, and their swan-garments lay beside them. The brothers took them home with them to be their wives: Egil took *Olrun*, Slagfith took *Svanhvit*, and Volund, *Alvitr*.

VKV. 4

Later they sat   seven winters together
but in the eighth   they pined throughout,
and in the ninth   they needs must part;
the maidens longed for the dark wood—
Alvitr[4] young   to practice war.

They were seized by their Valkyr-nature, which drove them irresistibly into battle. The brothers came home from the hunt, but found the rooms empty however much they sought:

VKV. 6

Eastward strode Egil   for Olrun
and southward Slagfith   for Swanwhite,
But Volund alone   in Wolfdale sat.

---

[1]Lament of Deor.
[2]Valleys of the Wolf (Wolfdale).
[3]Wolf-Lake.
[4]"The heavenly young maidens" is suggested for *Alvitr*.

VKV. 7

He set in red gold   the precious stone,
wound all   the rings with linden-bast:
thus did await his   . . . shining
wife, if to him   she would come again.

16. NITHUTH.—The Niara king Nithuth now hears that Volund
is dwelling alone in the Wolf-Dales and has gold and costly things
in abundance, which he fashions with great skill. The avaricious
king now places himself in ambush at night-time in Volund's
house. When Volund returns from the hunt he counts as usual
the gold rings he has hanging on a fibre-cord under the roof, and
one is missing—the one Nithuth has taken. Volund's first thought
is that his wife perhaps has returned home, but since no one is to
be seen he falls asleep. He is overcome and bound by the king
and his men. Upon the queen's advice they cut the tendons of his
ankles and set him as a cripple out on the island *Saevarstath*,
where he must forge precious things for the king, and he may be
visited by him alone. Then Volund sings:

VKV. 19

There shone Nithuth's   sword at his girdle,
that which I whetted   skillfully as I was able
(and I hardened it   as most fitting seemed)
this shining sword,   borne far from me for aye.

20

He sat, he slept not, unceasing beat his hammer,
his art he plied right   speedily for Nithuth.

17. REVENGE.—Nor was vengeance long delayed. The two
sons of the avaricious king stole in upon Saevarstath to get gold
for themselves, but Volund outwitted and slew them. Their
skulls he covered with silver and sent them to Nithuth for drinking-cups; of their eyes he fashioned jewels for the queen, and of
their teeth a breast-ornament for her daughter, Bothvild.

A short time afterwards Bothvild broke a costly ring which her
father had given her. She dared not confess to him her misfortune and appealed to Volund to have the damage repaired. He
received her kindly and promised to repair the ring; but after he
had brought her to a seat and stupefied her with strong drink, he

dishonored the king's daughter as a climax to his terrible revenge. At the same time his skill was put to a good test; he had made himself a feather cloak so as to fly away from the island:

VKV. 31

Laughing Volund   rose in air,
weeping Bothvild   passed from the isle.

The conclusion of the poem is incomplete and obscure. Volund's gifts occasion disturbance in the king's court. Neither the king nor the queen can sleep; they tremble in fever and distrust each other. It seems that Volund had flown hither to the castle and with scornful words described the trouble he had caused. Nithuth answered:

VKV. 39

You spoke no word   which would grieve me worse,
I will not, Volund,   blame thee more;
no man is there so tall   as to take thee from thy horse
nor yet so strong   that he might shoot thee down,
there where you soar   against the clouds.

40

Laughing Volund   rose in air,
but joyless Nithuth   sat there then.

The song ends with Nithuth having his daughter called, and she confirms the story of what has happened.—From other sources we know that the child of Volund and Bothvild was a son, *Witige;* he appears very commonly in our Danish folk-songs under the name of *Vidrik, Verland's* son.

THE HJATHNINGAR[1]

18. THE PEACE OF FROTHI.—We have already mentioned the myth telling how the end of the Golden Age, occasioned by the struggle between the Aesir and the Vanir, was prepared in various ways: the three giant maids come to Asgarth, that is, the Valkyrs (or Norns) who give warning of the coming battle. This transition from the original peaceful condition of happiness and

----

[1]Or the Hjathnings.

innocence to times of warfare is pictured in several mythical and semi-heroic poems in the works of Saxo and of Icelandic authors. Saxo thus gives an account of the prosperous reign of "Peace-Frothi," when there was such complete peace in the country that one could lay gold upon the highway without its being stolen. About this "Peace of Frothi" the Eddic Song, *Grotta-songr*, and also Snorri relate the following:

The Danish king *Frothi* visited King *Fjolnir* in Sweden and at his house he bought, on departing, two large, strong bond-women, *Fenja* and *Menja*. At the same time there were found in Denmark two large hand-mills driven ashore. No one had the strength to turn them, although they could grind everything which one might desire. Whoever had stones in his possession put them into a mill which he called *Grotti* and brought it to King Frothi. He then set his strong bondwomen to grinding; they took no rest and he heard them continually singing at the mill. Menja quoth:

GROTT. 5

Wealth let us grind for Frothi,   let us grind most happy
mass of riches let us grind   in fortune's mill.
He sat upon the riches,   he slept upon the down,
let him awake to wish,   then it is well ground.

6

Here shall no one   hurt the other,
prepare his harm   or plan his death,
or strike with the   sharp sword,
though his brother   find in bonds.

For all that the king would not give them the needful rest. "You must not sleep beyond the hour when the cuckoo's note sounds over the hall." Fenja and Menja rebuked him for his folly; they told him that they were mighty and ancient giantesses who already had occasioned great discord in the world. Now they were grinding war and public calamity for the kingdom: "Frothi shall lose the throne of *Hleithr*,[1] but Yrsa's son[2] shall later take vengeance for the murder of *Halfdan*."

[1]Now Lejre, in Zealand.
[2]Hrolf-Kraki.

GROTT. 23

The maidens ground,   applied their strength
were young   in giant power;
the poles shook,   the casing fell,
and then burst the heavy   block asunder and in twain.

19. THE BRISING ORNAMENT.—Odin loved Freyja. (She was
his *frithla*, his 'beloved,' consequently is confused with Frigg.)
One day she came to a stone where there lived four dwarfs who
had prepared a very handsome necklace of gold. The goddess
would have been glad to gain this, but the dwarfs demanded and
insisted that her love should be the price; so the ornament was
dearly bought before she could call it her own. Meanwhile the
crafty Loki had learned of the matter and immediately impart-
ed his knowledge to Odin. The latter commanded him to seize
the ornament from Freyja and bring it to him; and this was
done, but not without some difficulty. In order to get the necklace back Freyja had to promise to make discord between two
kings who were so mighty that twelve kings served under them,
and this conflict was to last forever. Then began the Njathning-
Storm, *i.e.* the Battle.

Hjathning Battle.—Hethin, king of Norway, carried away Hild,
daughter of the Danish king Hogni, who at that time was on a
warlike expedition. When the latter returned shortly after
Hethin's plundering, he fitted out his fleet, pursued the thief, and
overtook him. It was in vain that Hild sought to effect a reconciliation between her father and her lover, although she offered her
father in amends a costly necklace. The battle began; Hogni and
Hethin slew each other, and there was great slaughter on both
sides. Every night Hild with her enchantments awoke the fallen
heroes to life again. The following morning the strife would begin
anew, and so it was to continue until Ragnarok.

This Saga of the Hjathnings wandered in Viking times to England
and the Netherlands, where it soon became very popular. From the
Netherlands it became known in Germany, where at about the same
time as the Nibelungenlied (about 1200) there was composed a great
hero-poem, Gudrun,[1] on the basis of this Northern theme.

---

[1] Or Kudrun.

BEOWULF

20. THE LAY OF BEOWULF.—The sagas of Beowulf, according to the opinion of most scholars, had their home and origin in Sweden or Denmark. Now they are found only in an Anglo-Saxon art-poem dating from the beginning of the eighth century; but since the original foundation is Northern, we will relate briefly the chief points of the poem.

The Danish king *Hrothgar* had a splendid hall built for himself in which he wished to hold his feasts. But at this the troll *Grendel* became much embittered, and creeping at night into the king's hall seized thirty of the king's men. Since this recurred night after night, there were anxiety and despair in the whole realm. The report of Grendel's crime also reached the Geats, whose best man, Beowulf, at the head of chosen warriors resolved to hasten to the help of the Danish king. He was received with homage and exaltation and a great feast. In the evening he and his men remained behind in the hall alone, where Grendel as usual appeared and seized one of the Geats, whom he tore in sunder. Beowulf, however, drew his sword and after a frightful combat cut off the right arm of the troll and put him to flight.

21. GRENDEL'S MOTHER.—The Danes rejoice. But the following night the troll's mother comes to avenge her son. She succeeds in dragging away Æschere, King Hrothgar's best friend. Then Beowulf resolves, with the united Danes and Geats, to visit the troll in his own house. This is in a mighty swamp, which is so deep that Beowulf needs fully twenty-four hours to complete his wanderings. At the bottom he finds Grendel and his mother in a light and airy cave. A wild conflict immediately ensues between the mother and Beowulf, but his sword does not bite upon the invulnerable troll-woman. He then takes up a giant sword which is hanging in the cave and fells the monster. Hrothgar has meanwhile believed him dead and has marched away with his army. There is therefore great rejoicing when he returns as victor to the surface of the earth.

22. Now fifty years pass away. Beowulf has long since returned to his country and has become its king. Then in his old age a mighty dragon begins to ravage his land, and now he must

once more equip himself for strife. He succeeds in felling the dragon, but soon afterwards he himself expires from his wounds.

Into the chief action of this poem there is strewn a number of war-adventures and battle-pictures which we shall here pass over.

————————————————

Besides the individual saga-cycles briefly treated here,—those which have played an especially prominent rôle in popular belief and poetry,—there is found a rich variety of half-mythological, half-historical hero-sagas. To know these we must read the first nine books of Saxo, and also the Icelandic sagas. By way of example we may name the Danish *Siklinge*[1] Saga (*Hagbard and Signe*); the tales about *Skjold* (and the *Skjoldungar*), *Hrolf Kraki*, and *Ragnar Lothbrok;* the Saga of *Hervor* and *Hejthrek*, that of *Orvarodd;* and finally the Sagas of *Starkath* or *Staerkodder*, who has been celebrated in the songs of all the people of the North.

—————————

[1]Icel. Siklingar, the 'Siklings,' a royal race.

CONCLUSION

Since we have brought out in the foregoing the chief points of our forefathers' belief we shall now cast a glance in conclusion upon the conception of life among the Northern people of the pagan age, which has stamped itself upon their mythology and poetry, particularly as it is presented in the renowned lay *Havamal,* 'The Saying of the Exalted One,' *i.e.* Odin.

The gods are really more excellent than men but suffer from the latter's faults and weaknesses. Men are to believe in the gods and sacrifice to them; but these in turn *must* protect men, who otherwise soon learn to believe in troll-beings or "in their own strength." The whole character of the Norseman's life is permeated with belief in *inevitable fate.* This belief gives him equipoise even in life's severest trials and prepares him to await death with coolness. But the conception is not blind or fantastic, so that men should let things take their course. One must with cold reflection and calm understanding choose and reject, before carrying out one's plans, and thus gain the happiness, riches, and respect which every one desires and ought to desire here in this life. Sigurth says to Fafnir, when he has pierced the latter's heart and is threatened with the curse of the gold: "Every man will possess wealth until his day comes; one day we shall indeed all die and fare from here to Hel."

Scorn for death is expressed with great power in Ragnar Lothbrok's death-song: "I am not troubled about death and I wish to meet it. The Disir whom Odin has sent to me from Herjar's hall invite me home. Gladly will I drink ale with the Aesir on the high seat. Ended are the hours of life. Laughing will I die."

Undaunted courage is man's best virtue. He fells his foes in cold blood; all artifices pass excepting the breaking of one's word. One must not be cruel where blood-vengeance is not at stake. The conquered foe shall be slain—or treated with magnanimity. The Northerner does not scoff like the Southerner, even the highly cultivated Greek, at the fallen hero who lies in the dust before him. One must be *steadfast in friendship, uncompromising in enmity.* Ethical ideas are expressed with all possible clearness:

HAV. 43
To his friend   a man shall be a friend,
to him and to his friend,
but of his foe   should no man
be the friend's   friend.

44
Know if you have a friend,   one whom you well trust
and would get good from him,
in thoughts you shall commune with him   and gifts exchange,
fare oft to visit him.

45
If you have another   whom you ill trust
yet would get good from him,
fair you shall speak with him   but false intend
and deceit repay with lies.

But respect for friendship can also make a very pretty expression:

HAV. 34
A long détour   'tis to an ill friend
though he dwell by the highway;
but to the good friend   straight paths extend
though one have traveled far.

One must be *faithful to his lord;* to deceive him is the greatest piece of treachery; yet at the same time men must preserve their independence and never submit to injustice. Then must one be *faithful in love,* faithful in the relation between man and woman. This is portrayed with great force; but the joy of love is only short-lived and often leads the hero and his bride to meet a tragic down-fall. The strongest bond in human life is, however, not love, but rather *family pride*. This tie is sacred and inviolable both among gods and men and develops a firm conviction as to the justifica-tion of blood-vengeance, and this is extended to embrace the whole family. Men slay in cold blood until their revengeful desires are satiated, but this must be observed; they stand by the act and take its consequences. If an act of killing is concealed, it is mur-der, and murderers, perjurers, and seducers are punished in the Serpent Hall on Nastrand, the "Death Shore."

Naturally enough the hero poems have given us strongly ide-alized hero types and female characters, which by no means cor-respond in every case with the realities among the foremost characters of all people. *Inflexible strength* stands as the foun-dation of character and involves much that is harsh and crude; but the many bright sides of the picture are equally prominent.

In earlier times these were overestimated; but we must not go to the opposite extreme, since it would be wrong to ourselves and the life of our forefathers simply to emphasize the crudities as they are described by Christian writers in the countries visit-ed by the Normans. We should measure by a historical standard and not judge ancient times solely by the standard of the pres-ent. So also in the case of the general life-truths as expressed in the Havamal. They are often small, delicate recommendations as to the "golden mean" in daily life, and the whole matter smacks strongly of Philistinism, to use a modern expression. But the same section of the poem containing this ends with the fol-lowing lines, and with these we also will close this presentation of our forefathers' belief:

HAV. 76

Cattle die, kinsmen die,
man himself dies at last.
But remembrance never dies,
where it is well gained.

77

Cattle die, kinsmen die,
man himself dies at last.

One thing that never dies, I know,
Judgment upon all the dead.

Such words are expressive of a standpoint of culture which deserves our attention and respect.

EDDIC POEMS

FROM WHICH THE ILLUSTRATIVE STROPHES
TRANSLATED FOR THIS BOOK ARE TAKEN

I. POEMS OF THE GODS.

Voluspá (Vsp.), 'The Volva's' or 'Sibyl's Prophecy.'

Hávamál (Hav.), 'The Sayings of Har,' the 'Exalted One.'

Vafthrúthnismál (Vafthr.), 'The Sayings of Vafthruthnir.'

Grimnismál (Grimn.), 'The Sayings of Grimnir.'

Skirnismál (Skm.), 'The Sayings of Skirnir'; also *For Skirnis*, 'Skirnir's Journey.'

Lokasenna (Lok.), 'The Loki Quarrel.'

Thrymskvitha (Thrkv.), 'The Lay of Thrym.'

Rigsthula (Rigsth.), 'The Lay of Rig.'

II. HERO POEMS.

Völundarkvitha (Vkv.), 'The Lay of Völund.'

Helgakvitha Hundingsbani (Helg. Hu.), 'The Lay of Helgi Hunding's Bane' or 'Slayer of Hunding.'

Gróttasöngr (Grott.), 'The Grotti Song' (The Song of the Magic Mill).

109

INDEX

The numbers refer to the pages.